BEDS
I HAVE
KNOWN

CONFESSIONS of a PASSIONATE
AMATEUR GARDENER

REVISED & EXPANDED

BEDS I HAVE KNOWN

by *Martha Smith*

CONFESSIONS of a PASSIONATE AMATEUR GARDENER

MOYER BELL
Wakefield, Rhode Island & London

Published by Moyer Bell

Cover illustration: Martie Holmer © 1997

The photographs are credited as follows: pages 129, 195,
and 311 provided courtesy of *Providence Journal-
Bulletin*; pages 21 and 47 by Martha Smith.

First Edition

**LIBRARY OF CONGRESS
CATALOGING-IN-PUBLICATION DATA**

Smith, Martha
    Beds I have known: confessions of a
passionate amateur gardener / by Martha
Smith.—2nd ed., revised and expanded.

    p.   cm.

1. Gardening—Humor. I. Title.
SB455.S783   1997
635'.0207—dc20   CIP
ISBN 1-55921-193-8 (pb)

Printed in the United States of America.
Distributed in North America by Publishers Group West,
P.O. Box 8843, Emeryville, CA 94662,
800-788-3123
(in California 510-658-3453)

In loving memory of

Frederick J. Benson

April 14, 1895 - October 1, 1996

CONTENTS

LIST OF ILLUSTRATIONS

ACKNOWLEDGMENTS

To Jennifer Moyer and Britt Bell for believing in the perennial appeal of this book and for recharging my creative batteries. To Aloyise Pomeroy, Maureen Croteau, and Mary Ellen Corbett, for their boundless love and support. To my cancer survivors' group—Marlene, Pat, Linda, and Monique. To the writing group—Edith Mathews, Tony D'Abrosca, Nicki Toler, Laura Hunt, and Sue Haigh—for keeping me on my toes. To Linda Marchetti for incredible insight and support. To all my gardening buddies who have shared so generously their plants and information, especially members of the Rhode Island Dahlia Society.

The following excellent reference sources: *The Practical Book of Outdoor Rose Growing*, by George C.Thomas, Jr.; *The Saturday Morning Gardener*, by Donald Wyman; the University of Rhode Island Agricultural Extension Service; Wayside Gardens, Schreiner's, Milager's Gardens, White Flower Farm, Park Seed, and Winterthur Museum & Gardens.

And with special gratitude to the late Emily Kimbrough, a grand role model whose writing affected me so profoundly all those years ago.

INTRODUCTION

A lot has happened since I first wrote *Beds I Have Known*, in 1990. I've moved on from my first, beloved, garden and in doing so felt pretty much like a desperate mother leaving her baby on the church doorstep. But I've also been tremendously restored by the power of starting the process all over again—and by learning about others who have spent lifetimes restoring old houses and reclaiming neglected gardens only to leave in order to tackle yet another massive project.

As I've embarked on new planting experiences and even gotten so adventuresome as to launch a water garden or two, I've been repeatedly reminded of the forgiveness of Mother Nature. If you accidentally dig up a flower, mistaking it for a weed, and then murmur a heartfelt apology and put it back, chances are good it will recover and not hold the whole sordid incident against you.

At this point, I'm on my third full-blown garden, a creation that I designed and that is planned to take me, by phases, into retirement. I'm living now in a Victorian cottage painted four shades of purple (wisteria clapboards, plum finials, dusty lavender trim, a fuchsia door), and everything in the garden was planted to complement that color scheme. I like to think of it as the Mae West Memorial Garden, a sort of blowsy, over-ripe affair crammed with luscious hibiscus, huge dahlias, violet gladioli, lilac lilies and roses cloaked in a heady perfume. Mae would have felt right at home here.

When I was in the process of buying this house there was not a single flower in the yard and so, being unable to stand the thought of spring without daffodils and tulips, I asked the owner if I could dig up a patch along the driveway and plant bulbs. This was before I even knew if my mortgage application would be approved. "If things don't work out," I said, "at least you'll have beautiful blooms in the spring." She gave permission rather wearily, the opinion that I was missing a few marbles written all over her face. (Who willingly buys flowers and plants them in a yard that isn't even theirs?) Things did, however, go according to plan and by Christmas I was happily ensconced in the soon-to-be purple house, contemplating nursery catalogues and making sketches on a legal pad.

That first spring I hired a guy to help me dig up and till three areas that I had neatly drawn as flower beds: One was a long horizontal border along the fence, a sun bed; the other two were thick half-moons on either side of a huge maple tree, definitely shady. As I was working peat moss and bagged topsoil into the undistinguished dirt, various of my new neighbors dropped by to make such useful observations as, "You'll never get anything to grow here," and "Jeez, that's back-breaking work you're doing!"

Grinding my teeth, I had two silent responses which were, respectively, "That's what YOU think," and "Yes, dammit, I know. It's MY back that's breaking."

Every year since I have expanded this little backyard Eden: first a brick patio, then a fountain by a low rock wall; then a doubling of the sun bed, the addition of a rose garden, and the installation of a second fountain whose gentle trickling can be heard from the serenity of a deck chair where I have collapsed after yet another day spent on my knees wielding a trowel.

Although many things are different, the basics stay the same: There is no such thing as good digging; you cannot have too much Ben-Gay in the medicine chest; a hungry squirrel when faced with yummy garden foliage is no longer one of those cute Disney characters; and a menopausal woman who has been weeding all afternoon is no one to trifle with.

When *Beds* first came out, a friend who had moved to Manhattan from Rhode Island said she thought the book was a love letter to New England, and maybe she was right. So it is with a bittersweet feeling that I must note the passing of four of the wonderful characters who were so much a part of that first book: Lorenzo

Kinney, the azalea man, who lived to be 100, just as predicted; Antoinetta Goodwin, the wonderfully colorful "chicken lady" who planted marigolds in traffic islands, at 83; Charles Daniel, the kindest person and most generous gardener I've ever known, in mid-life, after a fierce battle with cancer; and my dear little dog companion, Dinah, the queen of my heart, who could not be saved even by the best veterinarians at Tufts University. In my mind's eye I see them all happily tending heaven's wondrous gardens, Mr. Kinney in his trademark bow tie, Mrs. Goodwin wearing a broad-brimmed straw hat, and Charles with his faithful Airedale, Margo, at his side, and her best friend, Dinah.

When I am in the garden I feel close to them; indeed they are all around me. I see them in the flowers they first gave me as seedlings, in the blending of textures and fragrances they taught me about; I hear their words of congratulations when there's a horticultural triumph and their encouragement in moments of failure. Sometimes I think I hear a familiar bark of greeting when first I open the garden gate.

To me, gardens are the repositories of a lifetime's memories and love—the special spots where one person, working to make something beautiful happen, can feel the influence and the shared joy of those who were the mentors and friends—and are still the guiding spirits.

In this updated version of *Beds* you'll meet another batch of extraordinary folks who share vision, tenacity, volumes of knowledge and a great deal of fun. Me? I'm still a gardener, still a devoted student of gardening. Still a believer in the words of George Bernard Shaw that gardens are "the best place to seek God. . . ."

BEDS I HAVE KNOWN

CONFESSIONS of a PASSIONATE
AMATEUR GARDENER

THAT'S NOT MY PERFUME;
IT'S BEN-GAY

It's not as though you have any particular desire to become a gardener. I mean, would Demi Moore crawl around on all fours massaging manure into the ground around the marigolds? Would Princess Di?

Certainly not.

But one day you open a box of oat bran cereal and find it contain a bonus—a free package of seeds. In a desultory sort of way, you poke some holes in the ground beneath your kitchen window and toss in the seeds and promptly forget them.

And then something awful happens: They come up. Normal life is over. You will never again waft about in Chanel No. 5; you will spend the rest of your life reeking of Ben-Gay.

Drunk with the power of having made something *grow*, you become Ms. Greenjeans—you, a person who once watered a cactus to death; you, who yanked an entire patch of baby buttercups up, mistaking the foliage for clover.

In my case, it all started innocently enough, as these things do, when I bought three railroad ties and a couple of spreading yews from one of those seasonal garden centers that receive shipments in unmarked trucks in the dark of night and are staffed by horticultural morons like myself. In no time at all I was landscaping, sort of. And, before you could say Burpee, I'd entered the strange underworld of amateur gardening—as addictive as any drug cult, a network of flower junkies whose carefully guarded trade secrets are what young growers are drooling to learn. All I had to do was ask.

One minute you're minding your own business, sleeping in late on Saturday mornings and wondering if the neighborhood kid will show up to mow your lawn, which is largely brown and dying of neglect anyhow, and the next you're ordering truckloads of topsoil, scanning the ads for bargains on pine bark mulch, and using phrases like "herbaceous border," "moon garden," "blooming succulent," and "rampant spreader"—a term you previously thought only applied to the condition of your expanding midlife fanny.

You are corresponding, regularly, with Holland tulip suppliers and speaking by emergency telephone hotline to Carolina nurserymen whose instructions require a translator. (Before New Englanders attempt to communicate with Southerners, both parties should be required to take an English as a Second Language course.)

Even the language barrier does not keep you from your newfound passion because you are—face it, now—an addict.

Darwin and breeder tulips
border a garden walk

Soon you find yourself among other addicts, people who "know someone" who grows foolproof primroses, or querulous old gents (almost always named Hank) who, if they take a shine to you, will give you a bag of their own secret stash—compost mixed according to a formula handed down from the Revolutionary War.

During the past decade I've become a peat-moss-and-perennials junkie, barely able to control my late-winter need for a fix—the sight of early tulip bulbs bursting plump and pink through the March-hard earth.

I have known the agony of broken fingernails and cracked shins. I have gone through two pairs of expensive waterproof Wellington boots and worn out the knees on more pairs of pants than I care to recall, consigning them to an ever-increasing stack of "gardening clothes" that now exceed my real wardrobe.

I have hefted untold numbers of bags of decorative marble chips, pine nuggets, and Bossie's Best premium cow manure, schlepping them from store to car trunk, from car trunk to garden in an effort of will that, just recalling it, makes me long for a strong drink and a good cry. I've planted rose bushes in an *Orphans of the Storm* downpour, rushed about under the midnight moon in bathrobe and slippers to cover tender shoots from frost, walked crablike for twelve straight hours, digging out the perimeters of a new fall bed.

I have known the panic of Planter's Paralysis, that wretched realization that, when you sit down after a day spent using muscles in places left unmentioned in *Gray's Anatomy*, you will never, ever rise again. When, after a few weeks, they miss you at work and send a rescue party over to your house, they will find your grimy, humus-covered body welded to the Barcalounger like bad modern sculpture.

If your colleagues have a sense of humor, they may opt to carry you and the chair out to the garden and set you up there, figuring that even if you make a tacky sort of ornament, it's no worse than the bathtub across the street that's filled with scenes from the Old Testament.

Balancing out all of this anguish—and there are hidden rewards in gardening masochism—there has been the unspeakable joy of seeing a whole fenceline of gladioli waving their plum and peach-colored bells in proud salute. There has been the exquisite delight of seeing a single frail tendril of clematis grow and spread across an entire stone wall, blanketing it with soft cups of lavender. There has been the occasional hard-learned lesson of nature's renewal: the loss of a favorite rose, a plant whose scent was a perfumed memory of prom night, whose petals felt as satiny as a childhood Easter dress, followed by the discovery of a hardier strain, smelling nearly as sweet but not as fragile, able to survive cold winter.

". . .BLOOM THEIR HEARTS OUT. . ."

Gardening junkies are all too familiar with such highs and lows and would not trade them for anything—not fancy yachts or box seats at the World Series; not a wardrobe of designer clothes or a brand-new Ferrari in a shade that matches your eyes.

Just when winter appears interminable, and it seems not one more bleak and bitter day can be endured, the first harbinger of the gardener's spring arrives: the nursery catalogues! Out come sketch pads and order forms, and inspiring ideas like, "Yes! Some hydrangeas would be just the thing for that corner!" Presto—another season of mad addiction begins to have its way with the imagination and soul.

I, who smoked cigarettes and stopped, ate to excess and repented at Weight Watchers, and successfully practiced behavior modification on a number of other unpleasant traits, have at last found a compulsion to which I gladly surrender. I have submitted to the gardening urge and have found to my absolute amazement that I'm not half bad at it.

My theory is that the flowers, appreciating how hard I try, cannot bear to disappoint me and, therefore, bloom their hearts out in recognition of this devotion. In the plant world, I am like Smith Barney. I get my blisters the old-fashioned way: I earn them.

Gardening is a habit of which I hope never to be cured, one shared with an array of fascinating people who've helped me grow and bloom along with my flowers. My mother, who had a grand sense of humor if not much of a green thumb, used to display on her refrigerator door a cartoon showing a little old lady crawling around a pansy patch on all fours. More a commentary on the annoying limitations of growing old than of growing flowers, its caption read, "The hardest thing to raise in my garden is my knees."

And the easiest is the spirit.

IN THE COURT OF
JOHN THE DAHLIA KING

It was with horror, one day that fateful summer a few years back, that I overheard my seventy-year-old neighbor, John Northup, proudly telling friends, "Oh, yes! I'm the one who got Martha started in dahlias!"

I wanted to jump across the fence, fling myself into the peat moss at his feet, and tearfully beg him to take back his words.

"No, no!" I would gulp, writhing as one in the clutches of some dread disease, as indeed Dahlia Fever should be classified. "I'm not *really* started in dahlias. I only have a few. Just to try. Just a small experiment."

Of course, it wouldn't work. Once you've been "started in dahlias" (and it's all done by extremely nefarious methods, mind you), there's no escape. How could you ever again live without the showy beauty of the massive purple cactus-style blooms that give dazzle to a flower arrangement? How could you do without fresh-cut dahlias in an array of shapes, sizes, and colors from late spring straight through to hard frost, blooming and blooming, begging to be given away in bouquets to friends and colleagues?

Veteran dahlia growers are shameless in their pursuit of converts. They start by inviting you to view their gardens, cutting a few stunners for you, and then, as John did, casually offering some tubers to "get you started."

The next thing you know, you're in their thrall, victim of the dahlia's astonishing beauty, consigned to a lifetime of all the responsibility involved in producing that loveliness: tilling, planting, staking, pinching, measuring, fertilizing, irrigating, mulching, and, come the first frost, digging up and packing away indoors.

No wonder I wanted out—or at least thought I did—that first year of drudgery and error. What had I gotten myself into? How could I, with the botanical insights of a couch potato, have fallen victim to Dahlia Fever? One night when the mystery kept me awake, along with the pain of my blistered fingers and aching back, I mused about the whole matter and determined that John was to blame. It was he who introduced me to the heady business of serious gardening, that Other World filled with hyperactive hobbyists whose rewards are lavish compliments and show ribbons, and whose disappointments are beetle-chewed blossoms and prize tubers that die quietly in their boxes during the dark of winter.

And while I complain excessively about how John's influence has made me a slave to my garden, I confess I've been an eager Peeping Tom in *his* garden, furtively watching his every move. Much of what I first learned

DAHLIAS: 1 CACTUS, 2 SINGLE, 3 POMPON, 4 FORMAL
DECORATIVE, 5 INFORMAL DECORATIVE, 6 COLLARETTE,
7 ANEMONE-FLOWERED, 8 PEONY-FLOWERED

about growing, before he officially took me under his wing and transformed me into a dahliaphile, was simply the result of careful observation of his activities.

I was ripe for the seduction of gardening when I moved into a new house with a yard consisting of eighty percent rock and twenty percent sand. By contrast, just over the fence in John Northup's yard, was a paradise of miniature melon pompons, cactus-pointed blossoms of white, lavender, lemon chiffon, and lush scarlet silken to the touch.

Before I'd barely had a chance to move in, John popped his head over the fence to extend a cheery greeting and a gorgeous bouquet.

That day is forever etched in my memory, along with other equally catalytic events, such as the first time my mother said, "Have another piece of pie, dear. You can start your diet tomorrow."

It was one of those pivotal occasions when I made a life-changing decision to stop being an observer and to become a participant. There had been other things in life I'd longed to do—tap-dance, ice skate, paint gorgeous still lifes, become Miss America—but none of those goals was realistic.

You don't have to be pretty or artistic or agile to become a gardener. All you have to be is persistent—and spongelike when it comes to absorbing the information veteran growers are eager to share. And, while it's true my klutziness has led to many a garden mishap, only my pride has ever been seriously injured.

To his great credit, John has never laughed at my pratfalls in the garden, although he has gotten cranky when I've forgotten to label plants, an act of negligence he considers sinful. But, then, John is a perfectionist, especially when it comes to his beloved dahlias. He grows some 250 varieties, from the tiny, compact pom-pons to the giant Type A-class dahlias which span fourteen inches. A fierce competitor for a man with such a genial nature, he won his first flower-show ribbon in 1969 with a bronze, cactus-style dahlia called Smarty. At the age of seventy, he collected 250 awards in three states, including election to the Court of Honor, which is the equivalent of knighthood in dahliadom; and took blue ribbons in his first effort at the National Dahlia Show.

Nearly every balmy morning we'd chat across the back fence in our bathrobes. On some days, when all I could make of his conversation was, "Mmpph," John excused himself to go inside and insert his dentures. He is gray-haired and grizzled, his face a roadmap of lines through friendly terrain. He has a wry sense of humor and wears a baseball cap that says "Grow Dahlias!" (I favor an apron bearing the legend "Grow, Dammit!")

John, a die-hard Yankee, has an inordinate pride of place. He likes to point out that, except for a scenic tour of Europe during World War II, he's spent his entire life right here in South County, the southeastern tip of Rhode Island. Growing up in the quiet rural atmosphere of those bygone days of kitchen gardens, pet rabbits, and family chickens caused John to dream of making farming his life. "I grew my first tomato when I was six," he recalls, "and after that I was hooked on gardening."

Both his grandfathers were gardeners, but the genetic green thumb skipped a generation, missing John's parents and settling on him. After military service he earned a college degree in agricultural economy but discovered the profession didn't pay much. He went to work for a farm supply firm but quit in disgust when he found out the truck driver was making as much as he was. He left to become a production planner for Electric Boat, the huge submarine builder, and stayed thirty-two years, until he retired.

Along the way he has become a sort of rustic Renaissance man. Today he chops his own firewood, cleans and smokes fish caught by his seafaring sons, and cooks dinner for his wife, Joyce, who is unwell.

His urge to garden has remained insatiable. Not satisfied with just filling his own yard with vegetables and blossoms, he craves more planting space. Before my house was built, he cultivated the site for fifteen years.

"I hand-spaded the whole lot," he recalls. "I had it

half planted in vegetables and half in flowers, mostly annuals. When the land was sold and split up into house lots, they didn't even have to clear for your place. Every year Joyce would see me head next door with my axe and she'd yell, 'You're not clearing *more* garden are you?'

"I'd say, 'No!' . . . chop . . . chop . . . chop."

Then one day the contractors who built my house came along and stripped the rich, dark topsoil John had created over the years and replaced it with something called fill. By the time I moved into the place, my property could have passed for the Sahara.

Conan the Barbarian, working without a lunch break, couldn't rid my yard of the boulders, pebbles, and sand that had been hauled in to assure the house a dry basement. Undaunted, I spent a half-dozen years making inroads into the mess and buying truckloads of loam to recreate the fertile land that once existed here.

Today, the garden—faithfully enlarged every spring by a new planting project—completely surrounds the house. There are hedges of boxwood and English lavender set in as seedlings; and a dwarf McIntosh apple tree. The foliage of artemesia, lemon thyme, hosta, and St. John's cross abounds, as do the flowers of achillea, lilies, irises, vining clematis, anemone, and astilbe. Hydrangeas that were once houseplant-size now spread their arms and wave their pompons like a large cheer-

JOHN NORTHUP

leading squad. A pretty weed called golden glow, once barely six inches, now surpasses seven feet.

One day, while I sweated over one of my new planting sites, I hit pay dirt! In went the shovel, out came the distinctive aroma of Eau de Cow. I had uncovered a remnant of John's old garden. Naturally, this treasure trove of soil is where I decided to plant the prize dahlia tubers he had given me.

Today, the finicky dahlias thrive there, a loud and unruly lot of colorful characters each trying to be the tallest, brightest, or most admired. My two favorites are old-fashioned varieties—the rich plum-colored Thomas Edison and the candy-striped Connecticut Dancer, with its surprising patterns and ruby flecks.

Dahlias lend themselves to gift-giving because mature plants produce many baby plants by the end of every growing season. If you want to get *really* serious, you can go to dahlia root auctions and buy champion tubers or you can order unusual varieties from catalogues, but that's unnecessary if you know a successful grower like John. The original tuber, dug up in the fall, has sprouted multiple new tubers or "toes" which can be divided to form new plants. If you store them snugly during the winter, when they emerge in the spring they will be dotted with little sprouts resembling potato eyes—enough for yourself and friends.

And neighbors. And co-workers. And total strangers.

Another nice thing about dahlias is that they will bloom profusely all summer if you follow John's recommendations. Plant them in a rich, well-drained soil, far enough apart so the foliage has room to stretch its arms, and make sure they get lots of sun. I fertilize from bags of mix labeled with numbers that sound as if they open gym lockers. All I know is what John and other experts assure me is dahlia gospel: 5–10–10 is good for strong root development while 10–10–10 makes lusher leaves. For a rank amateur like me, interested in bouquets and not blue ribbons, abundance is what I crave, so I go for the lush-leaf formula.

Once the first frost hits, it's time to dig up the dahlias and put them away for winter's dormancy. This is the tricky part.

Unlike tulips and other bulbs, dahlias aren't winter-hardy. If left in the ground, they freeze, thaw, and dissolve into a stinky, pulpy mess.

There is certain basic information about dahlia storage. They need to be dry but not too dry; cool but not cold. They must be kept in a temperature above thirty-two degrees, with forty-four the ideal. They are susceptible to all sorts of rot and spreading fungus and, if they're stored together, these dread diseases can sweep through and wipe out the entire batch. That said, it must also be noted that nobody agrees on the best methods of achieving these conditions.

If three dahlia growers get together—as they did when John's pals Harry and Walter showed up to help him with the packing—they either elect officers or start arguing about whose storage system is the best.

"Geez," said Walter, rolling his eyes in annoyance at the piles of tubers stacked up on tables and pallets all over the yard. "What a disaster! These over here don't even have tags . . . do you have *any* idea what they are?" Walter, who speaks in Ralph Kramden-like declarations and is never without his baseball cap and portable coffee cup, approaches the business of dahlia storage as a sort of mystic ritual. After he digs them up, he washes the tubers as though they were Spode, then turns them upside down in a cardboard box, where he gently covers them with newspaper.

Other dahliaphiles, equally fervent about their own peculiar storage habits, use plastic bleach bottles, styrofoam, squiggles, and shredded computer paper for insulation.

John, a terrible procrastinator (he once left his tubers in the ground until it snowed), is more methodical about planting dahlias than about storing them. Full of enthusiasm in the spring, he rototills the soil for days, then crawls around on his hands and knees with tape measures, strings, and sticks meticulously labeled with flower names. By fall his enthusiasm has waned noticeably when it's time to dig them up.

(Despite his teachings, to this day I retain a uniformly cavalier attitude no matter what phase of gardening I'm tackling. Back then my little fox terrier, Dinah, would help by thrusting drool-covered latex squeaky toys in my face while I was working. Today her successor, Delia, assists by digging her own holes—never where I need them—and also by fetching the weeds I've thrown over my shoulder. Eventually all this aid causes me to give up, toss the bulbs in helter-skelter, and wish the bulbs good luck. Then I call it a day.)

Although John is infinitely more fastidious, his methods did not suit Walter, who threw up his hands, leaving mild-mannered Harry to bustle around, clucking ever so softly under his breath as he tagged plants for their winter boxes. After five hours, dozens of cups of coffee and extensive criticism, Walter and Harry wandered off, leaving John to his own devices—and still debating the efficiency of packing tubers in vermiculite versus dry newspaper.

The next morning Walter returned with one of those cardboard crowns given to kids by Burger King. He had glued faded dahlia blossoms to each point and penned in "John the Dahlia King" across the front.

"I thought we should have a coronation before you keel over in this mess," he explained.

"Say, Walt," John said by way of thanks, "would you like to take some of these home?"

There's hardly been an occasion when I haven't gleaned something valuable about gardening and life from John. During Walter and Harry's fractious visit, I learned that it's *extremely* important to keep a sense of humor—even if you're tempted to strangle your buddies.

Under John's tutelage I've come to realize that all gardening is trial and error: You plant something and, if you're not wild about its texture, size, or hue, you either leave it in the ground to rot (as I did with some hideous canna lilies) or you dig it up and offer it to someone who will provide the enthusiasm you can't muster. I opted for the latter course with a huge fire-engine-red dahlia that looked positively obscene among my pastels but was much admired by a neighbor with a fondness for large blooms in the primary colors.

I've also learned there's no such thing as owning too many gardening reference books and, more importantly, that it's vital to spend as much time as possible in the company of people like John the Dahlia King and other "natural growers." These walking encyclopedias will, with very little prompting, divulge trade secrets that, if you adopt them as your own, bring you success in your own fledgling efforts. This, in turn, will cause all your citified friends to gush over your bouquets and proclaim they don't know *how* you do it.

I confess to being a failure at one aspect of dahlia growing and that's the selective nipping back of buds so that fewer, more impressively formed flowers result. No matter how many times John assures me that it's standard practice among competitive growers, I can't get past the notion that I'm murdering baby blooms. I have decided to limit my nipping to evening cocktails.

By contrast, John never has too many flowers, but rather just enough, and that's because he coolly sacrifices certain buds for the sake of the show ring. He prefers blue ribbons and trophies to a rampant sea of blossoms.

"You had quite a lot of flowers this year, *quite* a lot," he observed, looking at the unruly remnants of my dahlia bed. "If you'd only pinched back, you might have put this one here in the show. This one is a pretty nice dahlia."

I did one of those sputtering coffee spits that Danny Thomas perfected on *Make Room for Daddy*.

"What do you mean this *one*?" I demanded, waving my hand at the three dozen other dahlias that had been so coldly dismissed. "I think they're *all* nice! They may be a little overdone in terms of how I let the blossoms run wild, but I like them that way."

(I do get a little defensive about my flowers, especially when there's a hint of disapproval at their slightly blowsy abundance.)

"There's nothing wrong with just letting them grow the way you did," John quickly added. "It looks real nice from the road and you've always got some to cut if you need a bouquet real fast."

Then, patting my shoulder, he awarded me the Yankee equivalent of the Medal of Honor. "You did *very well* for your first year," he declared. "*Very well.*"

I FOUND IT
IN MY OTHER GENES

I was not totally unprepared for my midlife discovery of the joy of gardening. As a child growing up in a blue-collar family in northern West Virginia, I gained an inkling of what the growing bug was all about by watching my parents.

My mother's concept of gardening might be termed single-digit planting. Every spring she'd sit on our back stoop, surrounded by flats of annuals and, using her right index finger, point to where she wanted the flowers planted. Then my father planted them.

"Here?" he'd ask, hovering over the spot.

"A little more to the right," she'd command, pointing.

A short, chubby female version of General Patton, my mother used her index finger to accomplish a number of chores. She found, for instance, that the act of standing in the middle of the living room and pointing at the piano was enough to send a tardy nine-year-old scurrying to practice her scales. She used the index finger method to train husband, child, and pets alike. I'm not sure what magic she possessed in her definitively pointed digit, but I can recall quite clearly that worse than seeing the finger direct my attention to some uncompleted task was the fear that she might actually start to waggle it—a sure sign of displeasure.

My mother liked getting results with her own two hands, except when it came to plants. Then, she preferred to supervise. A professional printer by trade and a pioneer among women in a male-dominated field, having started in the early 1930s, Mom was always more comfortable with ink than potting soil. Along our street of tidy cottages, neighbors voted her pitiful houseplants "Least Likely to Survive."

She acknowledged her black thumb and admitted that the natural disciple of Luther Burbank in our household was my dad, who worked as a maintenance man. My parents were much ahead of their time, particularly in rural Appalachia, which has a widely held reputation as a scenic but socially backward state. While my pre-Women's Lib mother excelled at a full-time job and also found time to bake and keep the house spotless, my father shared equally in household chores which included cooking a hot lunch for me each day when I walked home at noon from school.

While Dad was a fine cook and a willing cleaner's help, my father's true gifts were in the garden, and there, at least, my mother was glad to take a back seat. Born on a farm some sixteen miles outside our little riverfront town, he had the rural knack for making plants grow and attracting stray animals. Every home-

". . .CHILDHOOD WAS FULL OF FRUIT TREES. . ."

less pooch and injured woodland creature for miles around, made a beeline for our yard and his T.L.C. My early childhood was full of fruit trees, grapevines, vegetables, and makeshift hospital cages which housed wounded squirrels, orphaned field mice, and frail baby birds who'd been pushed from the nest.

My father's twin interests dovetailed to help him earn a reputation as the best grower of strawberries in the country. I kept a pet rabbit, a handsome salt-and-pepper-colored fellow named Jack Bunny—who was trained to hop by my side on a leash—and his droppings became the key ingredient in a rich compost recipe used to fertilize the strawberry patch.

Jack's donations to the compost heap were collected underneath the unique hutch my father had built for him—an elaborate structure resembling a combination birdcage and rabbit condominium. The back half, wood-paneled and insulated to keep out the wind, was lined with straw for warmth; the front section was floored with wire-mesh screen. As a thoughtful bonus, the elevated design of the cage put Jack and me on eye level so I could comfortably chat with him after school.

At five-foot three, my father towered over my five-foot-tall mother. A wiry man, predictably nicknamed Smitty by his pals, Dad was never much of a talker. That was fine because my Mom and I *were*, and he wouldn't have had much chance to get a word in anyhow. From time to time, however—especially during my difficult teenage years—he would share stories from his childhood that were designed to make me feel privileged by comparison. Mostly they were tales of youthful enterprise amid the hardship of Appalachian farm life.

He'd recall how, every Saturday morning, he'd make the long trek to town to sell produce at the farmers' market. At the end of the day he'd walk home, where nightly chores awaited him. It wasn't until I was older, long after his death, that I came to appreciate my father's rugged upbringing and his dedication to finishing tasks, no matter how challenging. Humility and diligence were qualities evident throughout his life, although it seems to me now that, like most children, I overlooked them in favor of real or imagined shortcomings.

Now I feel intensely proud of my parents, particularly of my father, who kept his dignity and self-respect in the face of economic struggles and deprivation. He had every right to be bitter, yet at the core of his nature was kindness. An orphan, raised with two other brothers by a teenage sister, he left grade school to work on the family farm. The early end to his formal education took its toll when he moved into the city and joined a work force of limited opportunity.

I can still remember him laboring painfully to sign his name to official documents like a driver's license or personal check. He spent hours each day struggling to read the newspaper. He read me bedtime stories, but with adult hindsight I now realize my mother helped him memorize them. As long as they involved rabbits and gardens, both he and I were content, although from time to time my four-year-old voice would complain, "You left part of it out."

"Well, how does it go?" he'd ask, letting me talk myself to sleep. I had memorized the Little Golden Books, too.

After I began dabbling with flowers as an adult, I was astonished to realize my dad had left me a legacy of a kind. I'd always known I shared his love of animals, but it came as a surprise to learn that at least some of his talents as a gardener had trickled down to me. I could not have been more amazed if documents had been produced showing I was the long-lost daughter of the Rockefellers, brought up in a simple mountain household after a hospital crib-switching incident.

Part of the surprise stems from the fact that, in virtually every other way, I am a carbon copy of my mother. Both of us could fairly be described as impatient, take-charge, terrier-like women whose notion of managing time alternates between furious hyperactivity and deep slumber. But now I realize that I am also like my father, able to summon previously hidden reserves of patience while waiting for plants to mature, willing to devote hours to the nasty job of plucking weeds from between thick spreads of ground cover.

I also share his deep reverence for nature—a credo that causes me to leave certain colorful weeds untouched and to provide proper burial for the field mice the cat hunts down and leaves in the tulip bed. Sometimes when I'm interring yet another deceased rodent, I remember the sickly baby robin my father buried in a tobacco-box coffin after unsuccessfully trying to nurse it back to health with a milky gruel fed from an eyedropper.

Since tracing my roots as a devoted amateur grower, there's not been a time when working in the garden failed to rally my spirits or remind me of distant days meandering down tall rows of corn, trying to keep my diminutive dad in sight as he strode off in his workboots, a hoe on his shoulder and a basket under his arm. Somehow, I still feel his presence and connection when I garden.

Dissatisfied with the skimpy bits of land around our house, my dad borrowed other plots of ground to sow sweet corn, hills of potatoes, and rows of vining squash and cucumbers, crops that all required lots of space.

If my father was the family's acknowledged gardening whiz, my mother was the canning queen, putting as much effort into preserving his harvest as he did in growing it. She would spend steamy summer afternoons over an archaic vegetable-slicer, a pressure-cooker with a menacing whistle, and vats of boiling water, turning out home-canned tomato juice, relish, bread-and-butter pickles, snapbeans, and whole kernel corn. It pleased her very much when her donated canned goods were the first to be snatched up at the church bazaar.

The memory of all her drudgery had a long-term effect on me. I do not bother to grow vegetables. The one year I tried, the plants sensed my heart wasn't in it and gave me green golf balls that masqueraded as tomatoes and lettuce so limp and brown it belonged in a hamster's cage.

I blame my mother for engendering this lifelong abhorrence of vegetables. We locked in combat for hours on end over the issue of my eating lima beans—green pellets that were slick on the outside and squishy inside. She would cajole, threaten, hide the disgusting legumes inside my applesauce, and, ultimately, insist I stay at the table until I'd cleaned my plate. I would still be there today if my father hadn't taken pity on me, and sneaked into the kitchen during these crises to scoop up and swallow the congealing mess.

Better times, etched in my mind like leaves on crystal stemware, were the quiet hours I spent in the garden with Dad, carrying a bucket or trowel. Sporting a Buster Brown haircut and red sneakers with my tee shirt and shorts, I would dig aimlessly between cornstalks and ask endless questions about what he was doing. Although he always answered, I'm sure there were moments when he wanted to throttle me for asking the same things repeatedly.

"What's this hairy stuff on the corn?" was a favorite.

"Silk," he'd say.

"What's it for?" I'd ask, vaguely aware that silk had something to do with my mother's best stockings.

"It gives the corn a topknot," my father would improvise.

"Why don't cucumbers have topknots?" I persisted.

"Because they're not corn," he explained.

Then he'd find a chore for me, something like counting all the squash hiding under their leaves. This usually kept me occupied until it was time to go.

When I was five he let me plant my own cucumber from a seed packet I'd bought at Baker's Hardware, using my quarter-a-week allowance. We carefully labeled it Martha's Cuke so nobody else could claim credit for the work of art I was sure would spring forth. Each evening I would run ahead of him, passing all the rows of corn, squash, and tomato plants until I came to the back of the garden where, in summers past, cucumber vines crept along the fence.

For the longest time nothing happened.

"When's it going to come up?" I demanded, my

lower lip forming the pout that never failed to get results.

"Now, honey," said Dad. "These things take time. Just give it another few days."

Sure enough, green shoots began to poke up and soon the vine was snaking across the garden's edge, covered with large furry-feeling green leaves.

And then one night it happened: A yellow-and-white flower appeared, shaped like the curl on top of a soft vanilla ice cream cone.

"Look!" I cried, dizzy with delight. "It's got a *thing* on it!"

The "*thing*," said Dad, would become a cucumber if I kept watering it diligently and watching to make sure bugs weren't nibbling on the leaves. (When I saw the first beetle and nearly fainted, he came to the rescue with a can of white dust that made the leaves look as though they'd been brushed with my mother's powder puff.)

As my father predicted, the flower gave way to a tiny green ball, dark and shiny and resembling an oversized marble. I watched as it began to expand, growing ever longer and fatter. A single cucumber grew from my plant, but what a specimen it was! By the time Dad allowed we'd better harvest the giant, it was roughly the size and texture of a fireplace log. Since I thought the object was to see how large the cucumber would grow, I was thrilled with the results. My dad hadn't the heart to tell me I had produced something totally inedible.

I kept my cucumber on display like a ship's model, on the windowsill beside the kitchen table, affording everyone a good view of a vegetable that was long past its peak of freshness. And then one night, when I was sound asleep, the Cucumber from Hell was quietly removed. I barely noticed because by then, heady with my gardening triumph, I had moved on to greener pastures.

I turned my hand to weeding, choosing an elderly neighbor's freshly planted petunia patch. One late July afternoon while my mother was busy in the kitchen, I wandered into the next yard and set to work. Regrettably, I couldn't differentiate between weeds and flowers so I wound up yanking everything from the soft soil. When I returned to the house, dirty but jubilant, my mother's eyebrows shot up and her terrier instincts took over. "Where have you been?" she demanded.

"I was over at Pop Lowe's," I said, referring to my adopted grandfather next door.

"How did your hands get so dirty?" she continued.

"I was helping him weed," I answered proudly.

"Was he with you?" asked my mother.

"Nope," I said happily. "It's a surprise."

My mother went out to inspect the carnage just as Dad's truck pulled up.

"Oh, my God!" she groaned, surveying the damage and then glaring at me as though she'd produced the Bad Seed.

"Now, Mom," said my father, as he approached and took in the situation. "I'm sure she didn't do it on purpose."

Sensing that my effort had not been the tremendous hit I'd envisioned, I edged toward him, fearful I had earned a dose of Mom's version of corporal punishment—a flyswatter smacked against my legs.

By now Pop Lowe had emerged, and, after one long, sad study of his ruined flowerbed and our tense family tableau, he burst into snorts of laughter.

"Well, if that don't beat all," he said. "Annie, come out here and look at what Muggins did." His wife appeared and soon sank down upon the front stoop, apron flung over her face, her shoulders shaking. I thought she was crying, so I started howling, too.

"We'll pay for the damage," my mother began, only to be interrupted. Pope Lowe grabbed me, wiped away my tears, and placed me beside him in front of the petunia bed. Then he had my mother take a snapshot that is still part of my childhood album.

If my botanical efforts went unheralded, my father's did not. His green thumb was most appreciated in late October when his pumpkin crop came in and I became the most popular kid at the Seneca Elementary School.

He would load the truck with his harvest and off we'd go to school, to hand out a pumpkin the size of a basketball to every student in my class.

After everyone had gotten one, our teacher, Miss Pansy Baker, supervised us as we carved what we believed to be scary jack-o'-lantern faces. It didn't even matter that my own effort was almost unrecognizable because I was on top of the world. During this one magical day I was forgiven for my thick, geeky glasses and my reluctance to play recess games that involved falling down.

When all the carving was done, the most talented art student drew a black pumpkin outline on a big sheet of orange construction paper and all the kids signed their names over the message, "Thank you, Mr. Smith." I basked in Dad's reflected glory then, and did so again many years later when, going through his things, I found all the homemade thank-you letters neatly bundled together in a box.

It turned out that my mother was relieved to see the truck leave with its load of pumpkins because it meant fewer pumpkin pies lined up on the kitchen counter. By the time Thanksgiving arrived a month later, she'd hit her pumpkin pie pain threshold and would admonish my father. "This is absolutely the *last year* we're raising pumpkins!"

She said this every year and every year my father's

truckload of pumpkins arrived at the school right on schedule. By the time the tradition ended when I moved up to junior high, my popularity had been secured by my willingness to let the handsomest (and dumbest) boy in class copy from my test papers. Pumpkins are nice, but they're no substitute for the name of the capital of North Dakota cheerfully supplied ten seconds before the bell rings.

As an adolescent, I was more interested in cultivating bad habits than flowers. My gardening career went on hiatus as I took up wisecracks, loud music, furtive smoking, and generally making my mother's life miserable. My idea of after-school fun was to lock the door to my room, put a record on the phonograph, and light up a mentholated Salem—a cigarette whose slim filtered length and faintly minty aroma seemed the ultimate in sophistication.

"You get out here this minute or I'm calling the Fire Department!" my mom would threaten, the Voice of Reality pounding on the door. I would turn up the volume on Spanky & Our Gang, my favorite '60s group, already blaring out *Like to Get to Know You*. Listening to their mellow harmonies, I'd puff away—careful not to inhale and ruin the sophisticated effect by throwing up. I would imagine myself Bette Davis, living glamorously in New York. When I finally returned from fantasy land, usually by suppertime, it was to an icy reception punctuated by the sound of pots and pans slammed into the sink and plates banged onto the table.

My father weathered this typically volatile teenage mother-daughter war by removing himself from the battleground. In summer he puttered around the yard in plaid shorts and shirts decorated with what appeared to be amoebas. In winter he took shelter in his basement workshop, sorting nuts and bolts into baby-food jars and bouillon-cube containers. Sometimes I would seek him out in his hideaway to mediate a particular controversy, usually involving an unrealistic curfew or my desire to possess car keys, and he'd behave as he had in the garden—listening patiently and saying little.

"Well, I have to go along with your mother," he'd usually tell me as I started back upstairs, but I felt his sympathy was with me. His loyalty necessarily lay with the other half of the parenting team, but the serenity of his companionship always seemed to soothe me anyhow.

Like a straggly seedling, I grew out of this unattractive stage, but, then, I'm sure he never doubted that I would. My father was an eternal optimist, especially when it came to things of nature—wounded birds, blighted plants, bratty kids.

A classic example of his never-say-die ideology involved a fifteen-foot walnut tree that he dug up in a foggy cloud of nostalgia, from the farm where he was

". . .ETCHED IN MY MIND LIKE LEAVES ON CRYSTAL
STEMWARE, WERE THE QUIET HOURS I SPENT
IN THE GARDEN WITH DAD. . ."

born, and transported to replant in our backyard. Even with her limited knowledge of the great outdoors, my mother realized that mature trees don't respond well to the shock of transplant—particularly when it involves such dramatic change. Our yard, near a noisy, exhaust-choked highway, could not have represented a more radical relocation for the country-bred tree.

"That thing will never make it," she predicted.

"Let's give her a chance," my father replied.

The walnut tree did not wither; nor did it thrive. It didn't do anything. For twenty-five years after Dad planted it, the tree sprouted new green leaves each spring but bore no fruit. In 1970, my father died of cancer, but the tree lived on.

In 1984 when I went home to visit my mother—by then frail, suffering from chronic heart disease, and near the end of her own life—we took what would be a final stroll arm-in-arm around the yard. There, under the walnut tree, were pounds of nuts that had fallen onto the ground. Still more were in the high branches.

My elfin, gray-haired mom looked slowly around her, then took a long hard stare upward into the proud tree.

"Well, I'll be damned," she said. "He got the last word after all."

DIRTY SECRETS OF A
MILD-MANNERED PROFESSOR

The perseverance my father showed in nurturing plants, knowing that eventually they would bloom or bear fruit, came as an acquired skill to me. Within my novice grower's heart lurked an impatient, green-eyed monster demanding instant gratification and lusting after the perfect gardens of some of my friends.

Clearly, I needed to learn how to *calm down* once I'd started gardening.

That help came from Charles and Violet Daniel, who take the long view in the garden, believing that all things come to those who wait and mulch. Both history teachers, they have a respect for the vast measure of time and the necessity of allowing things to evolve. Charles is a Renaissance scholar, an immense and consummately gentle man who lectures throughout the country. Violet, who reminds me of a modern-day Gibson Girl, is the most elegant gardener I know. She's the only person I've ever met who wears tailor-made suits and high heels to pull weeds. She's also expert in obscure periods of German history, her kitchen table littered with baffling textbooks that never fail to make me regret asking about them. The Daniels speak various languages and enjoy traveling abroad. Their idea of a really high old time is to spend three weeks in Europe photographing cathedrals and rummaging through documents in library basements.

From the moment I saw their garden, I wanted to relocate it in my own yard, using violence if necessary. Instead, I became the Daniels' friend and pupil. From them I learned that a garden, like a marriage, has rocky patches, but if you tend it faithfully it will provide endless fulfillment.

"We have a garden so we can get away from people," says Violet. "It's our own little park, private and full of beauty that sustains us."

The reason I visited the couple in the first place was to pick their brains on the subject of colonial architecture, not gardening. But it happened to be the height of summer and, to reach their door, I had to climb around a pile of zucchini stacked up like cord wood. A handwritten sign implored, "PLEASE Help Yourself." Subsequently I learned that Charles and Violet are compulsive donors. They've planted a flower garden in a vacant lot down the street with another sign inviting passersby to pick their own bouquets. They also grow tomatoes and dahlias behind a nearby church so neighbors can garnish a salad or fill out a dining table centerpiece on their way back from services.

It was only after I'd circumvented Mount Zucchini, walked around the side of the Daniels' red clapboarded

18th Century house, and wandered up the driveway that I saw their real garden. The sight of this beautifully planned and sculpted place, straight out of Colonial Williamsburg, was staggering.

Claret-colored Mister Lincoln and delicate pink Queen Elizabeth roses occupied neat square beds blanketed with pine bark slivers and surrounded by short boxwood hedges. A weathered fence served as backdrop for dahlias, hosta, flowering shrubs, gladioli, and low-growing annuals. Small marble cherubs and a bubbling fountain nestled among the centerpiece of the floral extravaganza—terraced beds of jigsaw-puzzle sections in a palette of rich purples, blush pink, and pure white linked by brick walkways.

Have I made myself clear? This garden was indecently lovely to behold. And there was more.

A kitchen garden overflowed with vegetables and herbs—all the necessary ingredients for Violet to make the gourmet meals that contribute to Charles's cheerful maintenance of his Henry VIII girth.

Other small beds carried out various color schemes: One near the sagging barn was golden, filled with zinnias, marigolds, snapdragons, mini-ball and pom-pon dahlias, and lemon thyme; another bed was subtle shades of ivory; near the back stoop, velvety coleus, pansies, petunias, and snapdragons blended in a riot of scarlet, burgundy and oxblood.

When I arrived, the Daniels were busy potting starter plants, gleaned from the excess of their own garden, to be given away to friends or, I soon discovered, total strangers.

"Welcome!" cried Charles, never having met me. "Would you like some hosta?"

"Yes!" I said, not knowing where I would plant it or if it would, in fact, survive.

For the Daniels, historians living in a two-century-old house, the only correct choice was a classic colonial garden. I was relieved at least to learn that they had spent twenty years plotting and planning to create their backyard paradise.

"When we moved here, the house was falling down and the garden was completely gone," says Charles. "Bamboo plants were growing eight feet into the yard; you couldn't even see the evergreens. On the site of the main garden, beside the barn, was a huge pile of coal cinders that had been dumped from the fireplaces. Every place I tried to plant flowers there were weeds and debris. We've been busy here ever since and we still find things to do.

"My feeling is that if we were to finish working on the house and garden we'd have to get divorced."

Charles and Violet understand each other. She knows, for instance, she will never break him of habits like leaving his brown leather gardening shoes out in the rain or using their best carving knife to cut up dahlia tubers. He knows not to undertake major projects such as plant relocation unless she's home. (He once tampered with a prize specimen Violet had coddled along and it died.)

True to her name, Violet likes to keep lots of purple scattered about and, with the lavender and statice she cuts and hangs to dry for use in making wreaths and arrangements, she's assured of having her favorite color year-round. Her most treasured flowers, though, are the roses, with their extravagant scents and old-fashioned charm. "If you prune them properly," she notes, "they keep on blooming all season."

Violet's gardening inspiration was her mother, whose passion was for homegrown fruits and vegetables. Today the art of canning is practically extinct, but it was an important household activity before the advent of frozen foods and microwave ovens.

"Canning was really the motivation for gardening in those days," she recalls. "My mother's canned peaches and apple butter were delicious—made from the fruit of our own trees. It was a source of pride to her as well as an economic necessity. There was a sense of self-sufficiency that came from having your own juicy tomatoes by the Fourth of July. That's why *I've* always grown tomatoes. When I think of it, the most expensive tomatoes I've ever eaten are the ones we grow here in this yard because of the property taxes we pay. It would be cheaper to buy them at the market, but it wouldn't be the same."

Charles got his start in gardening when he was a Boy Scout growing up in Missouri. "To earn my merit badge in botany, I went into the woods near our home and collected plants for specimens. After that I started my own wildflower garden with bloodroot, ginger, and other native plants, and it flourished, virtually untended, for years after I'd grown up and left home."

His father, a Johnny Appleseed type, had eighty or so fruit trees in the backyard. "Every time he heard about an experimental variety of fruit tree, he'd order one for the yard," Charles notes, adding that it was his father who inspired him to plant flowers on public land. "My dad and I planted poplar and ash trees on three empty lots near our house, and they're still there today."

For almost three decades, Charles has been distributing seeds and cuttings along stone walls on the back roads between his house and the university where he teaches, convinced that the sight of an unexpected blanket of blossoms will improve the disposition of the crankiest driver.

"If you stop and think about how little effort is involved, and the return you get in terms of beauty and satisfaction, more people ought to try it."

As a convert to growing, I am naturally timid when it

"Canning was really the motivation
for gardening in those days."

comes to slicing or moving something that could die if I botch the job. Charles and Violet have shown me that risk-taking is necessary: If you don't try to save a struggling plant by moving it to a place where it may thrive, it is surely doomed. If you don't thin overly abundant beds, some flowers will run rampant, choking out others; if you don't prune back the roses to what seem like brutally short nubbins, the bushes will not survive winter's ravages.

By watching Charles, I have begun to overcome my dread of tinkering with established plants. I've seen him reach down, in midconversation, to pinch the top foliage off a flower and then, using his index finger, dig a hole in the ground and stick in the small tendril. Within a week it is standing tall on its own and showing every sign of thriving.

Under the Daniels' tutelage, I have gradually increased my brave experiments. Some have worked and others haven't. When I fail, Charles offers me a new flower or tells me a funny story about his own mishaps.

Taking their cue, one day I mustered the courage to dig up a Peace rose that had barely managed one sad little blossom in an entire summer. After I moved it to a sunnier, less congested spot, it began to flourish and produce splendidly.

I experimented with cuttings, too, but had mixed results: The dozen tiny boxwood starts given to me by

Charles were all quickly at home and happy in new surroundings. But cuttings of hardy adult geraniums that I tried to nurture in pots under high-intensity lights during the winter promptly withered and died.

A particularly sweet-smelling rose whose scent reminded me of Victorian sachets did not survive its first winter because, after I'd pruned it back, I failed to cover its crown. I wept bitterly when, the next spring, it remained a skeletal twig, but Charles observed, "Some hybrid roses are so delicate that it doesn't really matter how much you try to protect them. You almost have to treat them as annuals."

Then, true to form, he told me how a very hardy old rose bush of his had kicked the bucket.

"One day last spring I noticed it looked sickly, so I gave it some bone meal. I checked for signs of blight, but nothing seemed to be wrong. By the end of summer it was dead. When I finally dug it up, I found that our dog (a buffalo-sized Airedale named Margo) had buried a huge rawhide bone under it. The plant's root system was ripped apart in the process, but because she'd covered everything up, I never noticed. I'm not sure what that says about which of us is smarter. Of course, I *did* find the bone and Margo didn't."

(While it's true that animals are naturally attracted to bone meal and will dig where it's been used, Margo is a nondiscriminating sort of dog with a sweet nature and

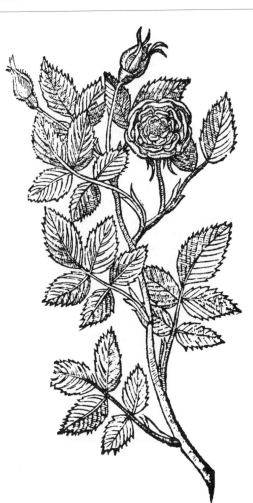

"...ONE DAY I MUSTERED THE COURAGE TO DIG UP A
PEACE ROSE THAT HAD BARELY MANAGED ONE SAD
LITTLE BLOSSOM. ...IT BEGAN TO FLOURISH."

the brain of a baked potato. She once tried to bury a bone in the bottom of a potted houseplant.)

Charles and Violet move about the garden as they do in life, at an unhurried yet purposeful pace, allowing plenty of time to savor the fruits of their work, usually from the vantage point of lawn chairs in the shade of their apple tree. It's a favorite spot to stop, rest, and sip lemonade while reviewing the unsolved mystery of precisely where it was that Charles put the sundial three years ago when he removed it for winter storage. He tucked it away so carefully that nobody has seen it since. Now, whenever he asks questions such as, "What do you suppose I did with my checkbook?" Violet replies, "It's probably with the sundial."

Unlike many younger gardeners, the Daniels proceed steadily, not frantically, towards goals. I'm grateful they've taught me to slow down. It's easy to get so caught up in the chores of weeding, pruning, watering, and fertilizing that you never sit back and actually enjoy the garden itself.

And once you've taken that minute to sit back it's time to get up again, because the most crucial gardening commandment is: Thou shalt not goof off. Finding something else to do in the garden—putting up a rose trellis, thinning out the coral bells, making a new shade bed in a shadowy section of lawn, buying a ridiculously expensive stone bench—all help maintain the sense of unfinished business that keeps us going long after our dwindling checkbook balance tells us to stop.

After all, a gardener with no dirty task looming ahead is an unhappy person. When other growers ask what you're working on, it's the ultimate disgrace to reply, "Nothing. It's all been done."

Charles Daniel died in December, 1994, at the indecently young age of 61, after a brave fight with pancreatic cancer. His colleagues at the University of Rhode Island paid tribute to him by hosting a "Celebration of the Humanities" in which poetry was read and a specially-commissioned requiem was performed. He was described as a man whose dedication to teaching was "an investment without measure."

The same could also be said of his steadfast loyalty and enormous gift for befriending everyone he met. Since he's been gone there hasn't been a day that I haven't thought of him and missed him terribly.

EVERYTHING YOU'VE EVER WANTED TO KNOW ABOUT SPECIALTY GARDENS

Rock Garden. So named because it's perfect for busy people such as rock stars who travel a great deal and don't have time for nasty chores like weeding. All you need are a lot of large rocks, which will thrive in any climate and never need watering.

Secret Garden. Favored by little old ladies who wear straw hats, print dresses in a cabbage rose motif, and white gloves to prune the floribunda, secret gardens have traditionally been secluded and unexpected beds tucked away behind stands of arborvitae. In recent years, however, secret gardens have become popular among indicted government officials who enjoy anything that has the appearance of furtiveness.

Gertrude Jekyll Garden. Named in honor of the renowned English gardener, this is a classic formal garden primarily using the colors of blue and white. Amateur gardeners often discover such a project is far too ambitious, leading to failure and the inevitable derision of neighbors. Then they must abandon their Jekyll and hide.

Herb Garden. The preferred garden of bachelors named Herb.

Victory Garden. These formal gardens, typically found on the estates of Wimbledon winners, exclusively use flowers that bloom in shades of gold, silver, and bronze, and employ loving cups and commemorative bowls as birdbaths.

Mary, Mary Quite Contrary Garden. Designed for the perpetually bad-tempered, this garden features flowering crab apple, bittersweet bushes, sour fig, prickly pear, rue and impatiens.

Perennial Border. Planted to honor houseguests who refuse to leave and therefore, like Sheridan Whiteside—*The Man Who Came to Dinner*—are destined to reappear endlessly, demanding nourishment.

Dish Garden. Indoor plantings named for nubile starlets of the '40s. Not to be confused with the Gish gardens grown by Lillian.

Moon Garden. The specialty of astrologists who only plant and tend the flower beds when their signs and planets are perfectly aligned.

Formal Gardens. Cultivated by those on the Social Register. White tie required.

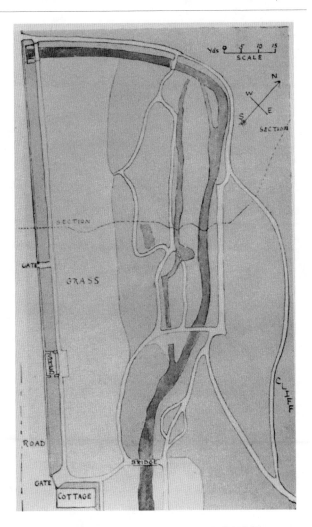

PLAN FOR MOUNTON, GERTRUDE JEKYLL

WHO YA CALLIN' YELLOW?
(DAYLILIES TO KNOCK
YOUR SOCKS OFF)

Even if you know where Tranquil Lake Nursery is, it's easy to miss. One minute you're humming down Route 44 in Massachusetts contemplating the subtle differences between Seekonk and Swansea and the next thing you know you've shot past the turn-off. I always say it's because River Street, where the nursery is located, is smack in the middle of a curve and, if you're heading east, you've got to cut across traffic.

The real reason is I'm already thinking about the spectacle that lies ahead.

In terms of dazzling floral beauty there is very little to equal the sight of Tranquil Lake's fields of Japanese and Siberian iris and exotic daylilies at the peak of bloom: acres of every shade of pastel, from the deepest wine to the palest pink. Several daylily hybridizers introduce their new plants through Tranquil Lake, the prestige models that cost a hundred bucks the first year they roll off the assembly line. Those, however, are not the mainstay of this nursery which caters to the full spectrum of gardeners from serious species collectors to budget-conscious hobbyists.

When you say the word daylily to most people they think "orange" or "yellow" and, after that, they think "boring." These are people who have not visited the splendid domain of Warren Leach and his partner, Philip Boucher.

The first time I went there, having received their catalogue and needing to see things for myself, I was dumbstruck which is, for me, a rarity. If you had tried to tell me that I'd become a daylilie junkie I would have told you that you could not have been more wrong. The colors yellow and orange have never appealed to me; I'm a purple sort of person, always have been.

Imagine my surprise at discovering that daylilies come in purple! And many shades at that, from deepest velvety plum to icy lavender. Once I found out, I was hooked. Now I'm adding to my daylily collection at a pace that almost surpasses the rate of expansion of my dahlia collection. Or, roughly, the hourly compounding of the national debt.

Warren himself acknowledges that it was a pastel daylily that knocked his socks off.

"The first time I saw really pink daylilies and lavender tones when everybody always thinks orange and yellow it was incredibly exciting. The colors are unreal. It's also the flower form: this trumpet-shaped flower. There are all different forms—round, star-shaped, all kinds of variations—but you'd get bored with a daisy. How many styles and colors are there? I like sunflowers,

Daylily

coreopsis, all the perennials, but if you're thinking of the complexity of flowers it's the trumpet form that adds to the appeal, adds a whole dimension of showing color on petals.

"You've got a green throat; the petals can have different textures and edges. You just can't get that diversity and interest in other flowers. Instead of nine buds, you have the potential of twenty-five on a flowerscape, having that long season of bloom."

As it turns out, before Warren and his partner bought the nursery from Charlie Trommer, in 1986, they already knew him because they were daylily customers. To further prove what a small world is the circle of gardening aficionados, when Warren was a kid growing up in Maine he bought plants from a local nurseryman and some of *them* came from Trommer, too.

"Phil White of Hermitage Gardens in Monroe, Maine actually got plants from Charlie. When I met Charlie I mentioned Phil," he recalls. As is the case with so many expert gardeners I've met, the earliest seeds of interest in what would become a lifelong passion were sown in early childhood.

"I've been gardening since I was five," he says. "My father died when I was six but he was a gardener; my great-aunt was a terrific gardener. There were gardens around our house that had been abandoned because my mother had four kids and she didn't have time to garden that much so I started trying to renovate plants that my grandmother had planted. My first grade teacher wrote on my report card: 'Keep up the botany.' That's documentation."

It was also a foretelling of what has been both a career and a personal passion. Leach subsequently earned a degree in landscape design and horticulture from the University of Maine at Orono. Besides his work as a nurseryman he also designs gardens on commission and teaches courses at colleges and horticultural societies; since 1991 Tranquil Lake has offered a lecture series.

"I've always taught classes at the Massachusetts Horticultural society, Arnold Arboretum and Worcester County Horticultural Society," he says, "but other than the Brown Learning Community and the master gardener program at the University of Rhode Island, there's not a lot in this area. Everything's up near Boston and Worcester. It seemed like a lot of people might be interested in talks and workshops."

And so they are. With a half-dozen lectures in spring and three in the fall, the nursery also offers other special events such as symposia bringing together experts from throughout the country to tackle a wide range of topics. The series has been a phenomenal success.

Large crowds, from total amateurs to veteran gardeners, will turn up for the talks which, besides Warren and his partner, Phil, often feature such nationally known figures as Jim Wilson, former host of *The Victory Garden* on PBS. Of course afterwards many stay to shop, wandering the fields of lilies and iris and poking around in the excellent inventory of hardy perennials.

Among the most popular of the talks was one on water gardening, a personal interest of Warren's. Living in Maine, he naturally became attracted to water and it was only a matter of time before he was trying to bring it into the garden.

"I first tried to make a water garden when I was twelve years old," he recalls. "I went to Agway, bought some instant concrete, dug a hole in the ground and lined it, and painted it green because it leaked. It eventually got filled in and turned into a bog garden."

I completely understand this fascination with water and the desire to have a small pond or fountain. The first year I began on my current garden, starting in a yard in which not a single flower grew, a priority was putting in a little fountain. I went to Home Depot, bought an oval horse-watering trough, came home and, with the aid of a neighbor's muscular teenage son, dug a hole in a corner near a short rock wall. In an antiques shop I found a nice cherub fountain, brought it home and hooked it up to a circulating pump.

Because it's located under a shrubby overhang from my neighbor's yard, the pool site is only good for shade plants so I've got solomon's seals and a variety of hosta there as well as my house plants who all get to go outside in the summer and get their feet wet—they're all sitting on flat rocks inside the pond.

Of course in my own inimitable fashion I did have to undergo one of those Baptist total-immersion rituals. It happened when I was down on hands and knees, reaching across the pond to align one of the rocks. The rock was wet and slippery, my hold was tenuous and— *sploosh!*—in I went, both arms wet up to my shoulders. My face was also drenched from the tidal wave effect of the crash.

In terms of design, if not necessarily execution, Warren approves of what I've done although it's a lot more like his efforts as a twelve-year-old than the extremely beautiful and complicated water gardens that are his landscaping sub-specialty now. This is okay by me: Mine is simple but it works and I've got just a touch of trickling water in the garden.

"In Maine," he notes, "there are so many natural pools formed from rock ledges. Water is always intriguing and gardeners have always been attracted to bringing water into the garden. There's so much—having the sound; it's amazing how a little bit of water can drown out traffic noises. Even if you don't have running water, the reflections of a still pool expand the space, make a small garden seem bigger."

As with most gardening, it's a good idea to think about the water you plan to add—make sketches, pace around the property—before you invest a lot of time and money in digging holes in the wrong spot. Says Warren, "It's much harder to make a naturalistic pool look real than it is to put in a formal or semi-formal pool. If you try to make something that looks like it came out of the wilds into your garden, that's a very hard thing to do. You have to have a lot of plants to pull it off. If you're using a liner you need a lot of plants to cover the edge. If you're making a naturalistic pool and you have a sloping yard obviously you should have your pool at the lower end of your property. With a formal pool, it can be anywhere; it can be elevated. If it's an elipse or a dog-leg, it doesn't have to be at the lowest level to look like nature.

"Pools are the ultimate low-maintenance gardening: You can go away on vacation and not have to water your plants. You get a lot of satisfaction. I don't fuss with filters. Filters have to be cleaned and I don't want to be a slave to a filter that has to be cleaned periodically. If you're going to have koi that's an entirely different thing because they put out a lot of nitrates. Goldfish and easy plants and oxygenating plants keep your water from turning green.

"It should be easy and simple and fun. If you're going to grow water lilies, you need at least a half day of sun; you can grow a lot of other plants around a pool without full sun."

Since they bought the nursery Warren and Phil have doubled the existing field production. The total nursery is twenty-two acres with roughly half of that in production fields. "I started making gardens and Phil started expanded the fields immediately," he says.

"Charlie mostly had a mail order nursery." This is the twenty-sixth year for the catalogue business. "It was anonymous as far as the site was. But I couldn't be without a garden so I began making beds in the fall of '86. It's more than just having plants. We can get excited about seeing daylilies bloom in the field but a garden is different because a garden is arrangements of plants but also arrangement of space and how you view it, being in it. You're in a nursery field but that may not be different from being in rows of corn—it's a mono-culture. The garden here is meant to be viewed from coming down the stairs."

Besides the daylilies, Japanese iris, and Siberian iris for which the nursery is renowned, Tranquil Lake raises some hostas and perennials; others are bought as small rooted plants and potted until they're mature enough

"POOLS ARE THE ULTIMATE
LOW-MAINTENANCE GARDENING. . ."

for re-sale. Others are purchased as mature plants for immediate turnover. The season is May through October and the catalogue division begins shipping at the end of April. The catalogue is produced and mailed by the first of the year.

Warren Leach likes to tell of a customer, an industrialist, who reluctantly came to Tranquil Lake for the first time at the insistence of his receptionist who thought he ought to see the daylilies. "Now he comes twice a week. He'll walk up and down and look at everything and we'll dig him one plant which he takes home. Later in the week he goes through the whole thing again looking for another plant to go with the first one. A lot of daylily breeders are either engineers or physicians, very focused people."

Of all the things I've learned from Warren Leach, not the least of which is that the daylily is the very foundation of a garden plan—and at my house, the more shades of purple daylily the better!—probably the most important is one of dynamics. He is able to articulate the gardener's interaction with his gardening space better than anyone I've talked to. Some people say it's where they go to be near God; others say it is a giant natural laboratory. Warren Leach says it is the purest form of partnership.

"How the space changes as you move through the

plants and how the plants change with the seasons create a garden dynamic," he says. "How we, as dynamic beings, interact is a dimension of living. Gardening people have relationships with gardens just as people have relationships with other people."

TERROR
IN THE TOOLSHED

Once you've officially got your gardener's learning permit and an army of well-meaning experts offering hopelessly confusing advice, there's only one thing more you need: tools. Make that three things: 1) tools; 2) money to buy tools; and 3) a place to store tools. Even as a beginner, I realized that my hand trowel was insufficient for transforming my yard into a modern bit of Eden.

Beginning a tool collection is like receiving a charm bracelet when you are fourteen. Once you get the first bauble, you can't wait to fill up every available space. You know you're in trouble when the clerk at the hardware store calls you by your first name and offers to push a large cart around behind you as you shop.

In short order, I had the essentials—spade, hoe, rake, wheelbarrow, gloves, etc. Then I branched out into more exotic equipment. First came a pair of Japanese cutting shears, a sort of Ginsu knife for plants. I have yet to meet a plant whose stem these scissors can't slice through. Next were shrubbery trimmers and pruning shears, followed by fancy metal plant tags guaranteed never to rust or to let your fancy Latin plant names wear off in foul weather.

While digging around the perimeter of my shade bed, under an overhanging deck, it occurred to me that I really needed an edger to neatly divide my flowers from the lawn. Not long afterward, I realized that the conical metal cages made to support tomato plants would be perfect for containing top-heavy lilies, so I ran out for a few dozen and then a few dozen more.

For the close work of digging weeds from around the rose bushes, a pronged fork was called for. When it was time to put in the spring bulbs, it was clear I couldn't do the job without a round wooden-handled scoop that extracts a cylinder of dirt, leaving a cavity exactly deep and wide enough to accommodate a bulb. Before long, one pointy shovel seemed insufficient, so I found a square-nosed mate to go with it. The single rake was lonely, too, so it was joined by a leaf rake and a narrow, fine-toothed rake which performed delicate procedures between congested rows.

Decorative stone creatures and white pickets followed, as did boxes of supportive vine staples to help hold up the clematis and climbing rose bushes. Next came the gasoline-powered weed-whacker, which cut down everything in sight with its lightning-fast killer twine. I soon learned that a small woman using this lethal appliance can accidentally level whole sections of redwood fence and fully grown trees before finding the

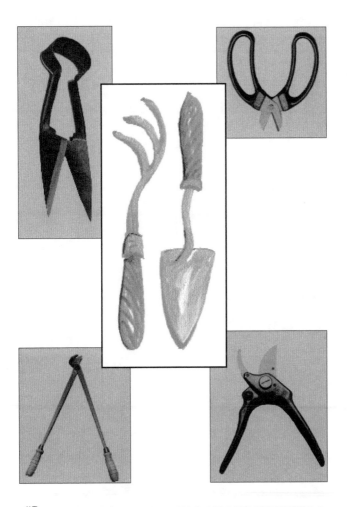

"BEGINNING A TOOL COLLECTION IS LIKE RECEIVING A
CHARM BRACELET. . .YOU CAN'T WAIT TO FILL UP
EVERY AVAILABLE SPACE."

off switch. After that experience, I surveyed my ruined yew bushes and packed the thing away forever.

The wretched weed-whacker was housed in that other gardening necessity, the toolshed. For me, the word "storage" conjures up images of handsome wood sheds resembling miniature barns, with window boxes in front and widow's walks on the roof. In my yard, this is not the case. Mine is the Toolshed That Time Forgot. And why? For three reasons: 1) It was on sale; 2) I put it up myself; and 3) after only a few seasons, it has matured into a pile of rusty, collapsing tin.

In my otherwise lovely garden, this abominable eyesore, containing any number of deadly weapons, should never have been built.

At least not by me, a person who is chronically uncoordinated. I was banished from tap dancing lessons at age six because my teacher got tired of watching me kick myself and my fellow pupils while attempting my version of the shuffle-ball-change. With this sort of history, it was a mistake to think I could erect a building.

It all started when I realized my tool collection had outgrown my furnace room, itself a crowded, dark place filled with a Rube Goldberg-like maze of pipes and dials. Leaving tools outdoors was, as I'd learned at my father's knee, intolerable.

So, scanning the ads one fine spring day, I discovered

that a local lumberyard was having a sale on a tin toolshed that came in a convenient do-it-yourself kit. It was of Japanese manufacture, but at the time I had no idea it had been designed by the grand master of torture, Torquemada. And so, I went out and bought the thing.

Back home, after I dragged the slim cardboard carton of components out of my car, I began humming the '70s feminist anthem *I Am Woman.* I was stepping where few women dare to tread, into that land traditionally reserved for the male of the species who laces up his Timberlands, hitches up his jeans, buckles on his tool belt, and struts off to do guy stuff.

My euphoria lasted only as long as it took me to glance through fourteen pages of assembly instructions written in some ancient tribal language. I realized I was surrounded by a surprising number of loose nuts, bolts, screws, and ancillary sections of sheet metal over which I had no control.

To my credit, I remained calm. I placed all the parts on the ground in an orderly fashion and refrained from serious swearing for at least a half-hour. There is, however, a limit to how long you can simply stare at a diagram and at parts and pieces which bear no resemblance to the artist's rendering. Sooner or later you have to wade in and start.

Assembling the frame—the metal strips forming the rectangular base with uprights protruding from each corner—was relatively simple. Then the wind picked up. There I was, a short woman on a rickety ladder in a forty-mile-per-hour breeze, trying to subdue a half-acre of tin. The experience was like windsurfing without the surf. I sailed about the yard, hoping to pass near enough the vertical support beams to bolt something into place.

After about ten hours of pounding, drilling, heaving, and cursing, I cried "Voila!"—actually I just said "to hell with it" since it had grown too dark to see—and pronounced the job done. At first glance, in the gloomy twilight, the shed didn't look too bad. I felt exhilarated at having completed such a task. I began to wonder why more women didn't go in for heavy construction and all its benefits of blisters, shredded fingernails, and the sort of pain experienced by pro quarterbacks who have just been body-slammed by a 300-pound tackle.

I got my answer the very next morning when I hobbled out into the light of day to admire my workmanship. What I saw was the world's ugliest and most embarrassing outbuilding swaying in the breeze. A neighbor, the local answer to I. M. Pei, walked by just then and offered his congratulations. "Hey, Smith!" he hollered. "Your shed's crooked."

In its first three days, before the metal doors buckled and fell off and bird droppings began to adorn the corrugated roof, I defiantly clung to the fantasy that I had erected a real building. I began to dream about acquiring more tools: A rototiller? John Deere tractor? Bulldozer and a backhoe?

Fortunately, my hardware store didn't stock these machines, so I settled for more mundane implements, all of which wound up in the murky recesses of the shed where no living thing save spiders and the occasional skunk ever set foot.

A kiddie wading pool with a tropical fish motif, purchased for my dog, Dinah, went into storage in the shed, next to a broken lawnmower that last saw service in 1962.

I began accumulating the small plastic pots that seedlings come in before you put them in the ground. (Gardeners are unable to throw these useless containers away. Every gardener I know has, at any given moment, roughly six hundred plastic pots in neat stacks somewhere on the premises.) My pots went in the shed along with the plastic flats nursery clerks use to pack pots of flowers and vegetables. Gardeners cannot part with these containers either, insisting that you never know when you're going to need one. You never need one.

Wooden plant stakes by the dozen were also tossed inside, adding to the chaos and upholding the growers' credo that there's no such thing as an oversupply of plant stakes.

By the end of its first summer, the toolshed was full

A SEEMLY TOOL SHED

of things I couldn't reach and had forgotten I owned, so when the next year rolled around I went out and bought duplicates.

Then I was back to square one, with nowhere to store my equipment, so I made the supreme sacrifice: I gave up a first-floor room in my house and filled it with more gardening impedimenta. Soon I could barely get through the door to that room. It was crammed with buckets and sections of wire fencing and baskets full of pencils, seed catalogues, notecards, plant tags, and half-empty bottles of weed killer or whiskey—I couldn't tell which from the door.

My toolshed remained a source of terror to me, a hard hat area to be ignored. Other hazards are unavoidable, however. I always seem to find ways to drop shovels on my toes and collide with wheelbarrows. I don't do it on purpose; it just sort of happens, much as the way I kicked myself out of dance class.

Take the creation of a rock garden, for instance. Where there is a rock garden, there are rocks. And where there are rocks, there are great expanses of hard, rough surfaces on which to bang your knees and squash your fingers. Putting the rocks in place may involve wrenching your back or finding yourself attached to an overloaded handtruck zooming out of control on a downhill slope. If the latter happens, as it did to me, you learn your limitations. I had to pick up all the rocks a second time.

I do try to take precautions in the garden. I wear high, sturdy boots to avoid slicing my shins with the hoe. I wear gloves to protect my hands and keep cuts and nicks to a minimum. But it is not possible to defend against *me*.

My worst gardening mishap, to date, involved a trusty water sprinkler and a circle of decorative fencing which I use to protect my dahlia bed from nibbling bunnies and roaming dogs.

It was a sultry summer evening and a young neighbor, a handsome and charming fellow, had come over to my yard for a visit with his girlfriend, a woman of considerable beauty and poise, on his arm. Naturally, I wanted to make a good impression as I rushed to greet them.

The sprinkler was on at the time, so I sought to avoid getting wet by jumping over the two-foot fence guarding the dahlias. I tried my patented hurdler's leap, clearing a height of about ten inches.

Down I went in full view of the visitors, my face scrunched in the turf in an ecstasy of pain and humiliation. During my descent, my knee smashed into a pointy-eared rabbit made of concrete. Meanwhile the sprinkler completed its inexorable rotation, soaking me to the skin.

This was not the worst of it. My foot remained jammed between two pickets, making me immobile in my agony. So not only did I have to face Ken and Barbie, I had to beg them to extricate me from my fence.

Later, as I applied iodine to my injured flesh and vodka to my damaged pride, I pondered how it's possible for someone as graceless as me to produce flowers so delicate. I decided that the plants bloom as a sort of consolation prize for my destiny of clumsiness.

A COMPLEAT GUIDE TO DESIGNER GARDENING ACCESSORIES

Laura Ashley Anti-Weed Sheets. Made of a heavy-duty chintz from her bedding collection, these go between the flower rows to suppress weeds and to make the chic statement: I've got an English garden, by God!

Ralph Lauren Country Tweed Gardening Gloves. Accessories for the gentleman gardener who wears them to complete his estate look—while supervising an army of hired laborers and not actually touching anything dirty himself.

Ralph Lauren Master-of-All-He-Surveys Brazilian Cowhide Gardening Boots. Worn with gloves, described above, and only while standing on the terrace. Never to be worn wading through mud.

Donna Karan Composter. Famous for making the simple yet elegant statement, Karan introduces the basic black composter with a variety of colorful lids that can be changed to match the seasons.

Tiffany Sterling Silver Watering Cans. Impossible to lift, but a stunning wedding gift for upscale gardeners.

Yves St. Laurent Gardening Breeches. Made of Italian leather, these are guaranteed never to wear out and if you get caught in the rain, never to unbend.

Elizabeth Taylor's Pest Passion. The woman who lent her name to a sultry perfume now sets her sights on an insecticide guaranteed to attract every male bug within 100 miles, then kill them. Eighty-five dollars an ounce; $40 purse size.

Perry Ellis Planters. They're chic, they're sporty, and they're madras plaid. Who but Perry Ellis could work such wonders with dull trees.

Gloria Peterbilt Heavy-duty Lawn Tractor. Gloria Vanderbilt joins forces with the Peterbilt equipment company to give women what they've always wanted: a tough yet feminine tractor with a wide seat, power steering, and pastel pedals.

Liz Claiborne Evening Flower Basket. For those who gather rosebuds after eight, this dainty container is of woven mesh and bugle beads. Comes with tiny flashlight and pruning shears, both gold.

Trump: The Garden Game. The ultimate after-hours amusement, the object is to grow the biggest vegetables and tallest flowers while simultaneously obliterating your neighbor's view.

Shirley MacLaine Vegetable Channeling Chart. For those who worry about whether their astrological signs are aligned properly to bring in a good crop of kale, the Hollywood star who has had so many previous lives that one of them may possibly have been Luther Burbank will personalize a chart for your garden. Just send Shirley your date of birth, a personal item that means a lot to you, such as your county fair blue ribbon for Best Artichoke, and a check or money order for $99.95, and she will devise your planting chart. While rubbing your ribbon she will seek inspiration from the various spirits of those now pushing up daisies and, via channeling, will decide where you should stick your zucchini.

Jane Fonda's Complete Garden Workout. Feeling tired and cranky after an afternoon's digging and weeding? You're probably using your muscles all wrong! Now, via her specialized videotape for flabby gardeners, Jane shows just how to bend and stretch and dig that weed and bend and stretch and dig that weed! Then, when you find the neighbor's dog stomping through your prize flowers, Jane helps you take your foot and lift and kick and lift and kick without pulling a hamstring. Later, just before you cool down, you can *"Go for the burn!"* by phoning the dog's owner and exercising your throat muscles.

PEONIES ENVY:
GARDENING ONE-UPMANSHIP
EXPLAINED

Jane Barclay is the only gardener I know who routinely takes photographs of her flowers and, at the flimsiest excuse, pulls them out for display in the same way new grandparents proudly unveil snapshots of baby.

I had gone into her gift shop to buy a vase to properly display my own blossoms.

"Is this for you or is it a gift?" she asked.

"It's for me," I said.

"Do you garden?" she continued, in what was the beginning of a friendship that would involve not only the exchange of photos, but fresh-cut bouquets and sob stories about visitors who had said hurtful things about our favorite plants. I bring her pink-tipped white gladioli mixed with the plum-and-white variegated ball dahlias. She brings me the fragile, blush-toned tiger lilies I don't have and sprays of bewitching bee balm, an old-fashioned thistle-like flower with a delicious, lingering scent.

It was after I declared myself a gardener—and long before I learned how little I really knew about it all— that Jane brought out her album and showed me photos of her trumpet lilies, as well as almost every other plant and shrub that grows in the Northeast. I felt like a "bad plant mother," which is Jane's term for those who act insufficiently proud of floral offspring.

Having nothing to show her in turn, I went home and started snapping pictures of my own garden. It has taken many years, but I now have compiled The Complete Pictorial Encyclopedia of Martha's Flowers, which, after three pages, has much the same effect as Novocain.

A candid photo of Jane snapped by her husband, Pat—a portrait that captured her studiously organizing the tiny office of her new boutique—inspired Jane to think about herself, and her garden, in a new light. She took her camera into the garden to extend this new perspective.

"When I first went into business, my desk was a $12.98 metal folding table stacked with papers. It was an awful mess and every time I looked at it I felt not only fatigue but futility. It made me think I was 'playing store' and not serious. One day, as I stared at the paperwork with my chin in my hands, Pat came along and took a snapshot. When I looked at it, I was startled because I didn't seem overwhelmed or bewildered. I looked preoccupied. I saw myself differently and it was a real turning point. The picture hardened my resolve to press on and make a success of things, to be as determined as I looked at that moment."

By "shooting her garden" on film, Jane also gained

"SEEING A FLOWER IN SOMEONE ELSE'S GARDEN AND
WANTING IT PASSIONATELY IS A POSITIVE THING."

fresh insight. "My mother would always say the garden looked nice and my neighbors would say it looked nice, but all I saw were the imperfections, and my own limitations. But when I saw my snapshots, I thought, 'This garden looks pretty nice.'"

I was amazed Jane needed her confidence bolstered in this way since, to me, she is the very model of poise and sophistication, always turned out attractively in tailored suits. She holds a master's degree in English—evidence of which decorates her conversation, delivered in a throaty Tallulah Bankhead voice. The fact that she grew up in Manhattan, surrounded by the witty friends of her mother, a book reviewer, also added to her worldliness.

Most gardeners are sensitive souls beneath the surface—but there are some insensitive ones, too. Drawing on her own gardening experiences, Jane has observed some of the less positive quirks of human nature.

"Passion and envy," she believes, "are two aspects of the same gardening instinct. Seeing a flower in someone else's garden and wanting it passionately is a positive thing. Envy *because* someone else has it is not. I've always been a passionate gardener and I'm thrilled by the success of others. I want to pick their brains to learn how they accomplished it! I would never want to be a jealous or envious gardener because it's such a terribly negative thing. I've had jealous people visit my own garden. I have found there's an ugly, nasty streak in someone who begrudges another's joy and beauty."

"Malice among the mums" first struck Jane when she moved into her house some years ago and was shocked to find that neighbors were vocal about what she chose to plant. "I never realized gardening was such *serious business*," she recalls. "I did it because I loved to grow flowers of every kind. But then I learned that people have rules they follow that say you shouldn't let daffodils naturalize themselves in waves over the yard, or that certain colors are gauche, or that dahlias are vulgar."

"*Not dahlias!*" I shrieked.

"Well," Jane comforted, "all flowers are vulgar in their own way. That's why they're not grass!"

Jane's garden is a riotous mix of old and new flowers, as well as those inherited from previous owners. She has the phlox that came with the house, a wisteria that isn't especially grand but refuses to die, yuccas that are mowed down every year yet still come up, lilies of the valley, violets, Star of Bethlehem, the enormous, exotic lilies, cousins of the amaryllis, that are her favorites, and Pendleton pinks—named for a college chum's father, an estate gardener who gave them to Jane for encouragement when she was facing final exams one spring.

"I ran out of room long ago," she sighs. "Of course, that doesn't stop me from ordering *everything* when the catalogues arrive. I also make the rounds of all the nurseries in the spring to buy other plants that I have no idea where to put."

Lilies are always on her shopping list.

"I can never make up my mind which new variety I want, so I order one of the cheap collections," she says. "I use the word 'cheap' advisedly because they're not. Once after getting interested in subtle shades of color, it occurred to me three years and two hundred dollars later that when a catalogue says 'apricot' or 'salmon,' it really means light orange or medium orange or orange-orange. I love the lilies anyway, for their form and their fragrance. I like to touch the raised freckles they get inside. And the best thing is that you just put them in the ground, they come up and bloom with no help, and everybody thinks you've done something terrific."

Because her freckled flowers are at their beauteous peak in mid- to late July, at the time of the birthdays of Jane's sister and next-door neighbor, Jane throws an annual lily party to celebrate the events. That's where her study of gardening human nature began in earnest.

"At my first party," she relates, "I had a man who sat in the midst of millions of flowers in bloom and declared 'Your lawn is all weeds.' And that was it! I wanted to say 'Leave and never return!' Later I found out he is one of those homeowners who believe all the blades of grass in the yard should be shamrock-green and exactly two inches high in case Jack Nicklaus shows up and wants to practice putting on it.

"The point is, it's very hard for gardeners to focus on *your* garden," she concludes. "Their response inevitably is about their own gardens because that's all they really care about."

She also observed that some of her guests tended to look at her plantings from six inches away. "They study individual specimens for flaws and end up missing the florist for the trees."

It's easy for nouveau gardeners to start thinking of themselves as great masters, adds Jane, who never considers herself anything more than fortunate when all the flowers bloom in perfect concert. She finds the business of growing similar to the art of making music.

"It's like taking piano lessons," she explains. "When you've mastered a two-part invention, you think 'That's not a mean accomplishment,' but, compared to Vladimir Horowitz, it *is* a mean accomplishment. You are simply not prepared to sit there with the whole orchestra."

A guest at one of her first lily parties behaved like an amateur Miss Marple surreptitiously poking her cane into the ground around Jane's perennials to be sure they weren't in pots, plunked in the ground merely for the occasion. Jane believes the people who pronounce dahlias "gaudy" or find her red and yellow annuals "vulgar" are overly influenced by the work of Gertrude Jekyll, the noted English writer who set the standard for perennial gardens in Victorian England.

"She was the one who declared that blues and drifts of white are refined and bright colors are garish," Jane explains. "I just can't do a garden that's planned and synchronized. What I have is a yard, you see, and the flowers decide where they want to be. I plant them where I think they'll look nice, and if they decide they don't like it there, I put them somewhere else."

When someone expresses distaste for something in another person's garden, says Jane, it's often an expression of his or her own failure. "There is a woman who said of my lilies, 'I hope *you* find those satisfactory. I tried them but didn't care for the results.' She wasn't really focused on my garden. She was conducting a little internal dialogue—a recounting of an experience of her own. From time to time, it's an expression of envy and even hostility, and that's when it becomes unpleasant.

"My guest list for the lily party has been carefully edited over the years!"

Jane became a self-contained person, happy with her choices in flowers and in life. A major influence was her great-aunt, who had an enchanting garden and an assertive personality.

"Aunt Annie gardened not for approval but for herself. She had a small city garden so she didn't waste space on the ordinary. I was only four when I visited so

I remember her flowers were at my eye level—I could sort of fall into them.

"She grew sweetpeas and honesty and in the winter used them in dried bouquets. She also made beautiful quilts with patterns sewn into them. She gave me quilts with creatures outlined in the quilting pattern on the back, where you expect to see routine stitching. In the middle of a sea of white she would sew a rabbit and in another spot, a cat. In other places were messages like 'Hello,' . . . 'Good luck,' . . . 'My darling.'"

One day, while strolling through a neighborhood full of charming gardens, Jane accidentally came upon the ultimate Yuppie Rehab Drop Dead Garden and was appalled to find herself being "vocal" about it.

"This garden was an exercise in artificial perfection," she says, recalling her disapproval even as she confesses her shame at being so judgmental. "Everything was in a variety whose color was so exotic you'd never see it growing naturally in this part of the country.

"The peonies weren't white or red, they were yellow; the poppies weren't orange, they were burgundy. You pay a lot of money for those things because the other colors are common. It's like drinking table wine—only peasants drink that; you drink Dom Perignon. Only peasants have orange poppies; yours are burgundy. Only peasants would be content with pink or white peonies.

These people had Japanese tree peonies that were in all the colors peonies don't ordinarily come in.

"I had to wonder what makes people want to have something so unnatural, so unreal? Why have white marigolds? There are other white flowers that are perfectly good, so why should marigolds be among them? Why create a marigold that's white and a petunia that's yellow?

"The answer is: 'Because naturally, it *isn't*. This garden had a kind of perfection of grooming and a vigilant searching for the unusual and the 'better.' The back fence was lined with what must have been $10,000 worth of espaliered pear trees—*effete! expensive!*"

Even though she would never dream of telling the show-off gardeners how offended she felt, privately Jane had no patience for this sort of horticultural snobbery.

"I can't stand gardens that are exercises in conspicuous consumption. It's the ultimate in vulgarity. It should be enough that you *like* the garden and it brings you joy."

After she'd finished her horrified examination of the excessive garden, Jane went home and took a reassuring stroll among her own flowers, which have never required anyone's official imprimatur to qualify as beautiful.

"This garden," she determined, "is pretty nice."

And she has the snapshots to prove it.

A GUIDE TO
GARDEN ETIQUETTE

- No matter how sincerely your neighbor says "help yourself" to his blue-ribbon roses, it is not polite to dig them up after dark and replant them in your own yard.

- Even if you are desperate for a date, it is gauche to spell out your phone number in decorative shrubbery.

- It is tacky to tell your spouse that trying to get rid of the witchweed reminds you a lot of the last time his/her mother came to visit.

- No matter how devoutly religious you are, it is never proper to anoint yourself from someone else's birdbath.

- If a guest's bratty kid is stomping all your loveliest blossoms into mush while his parent looks on passively, it is not permissible to pull up a stout plant stake and render him unconscious.

- Although you're still mourning your recently deceased hybrid tea rose, never wear a black armband to a garden party.

- If your hostess is an unmarried woman over forty, there is no need to attempt levity by announcing,

"Well, I guess these are the only bachelor's buttons *you* ever get to touch!"

- If you are attending a spring bulb party, it is not amusing to show up with a 60-watt Sylvania.
- Even if it is your party, refrain from pointing out how much the rat's tail cactus reminds you of your old boyfriend.
- Always wear white gloves to garden parties. In the event that you feel like stealing something, you won't leave fingerprints.

THE MOST PERPLEXING QUESTIONS THAT HAVE BAFFLED GARDENERS THROUGH THE AGES

1. Did *I* plant these bulbs here?
2. I wonder if I'll need a tetanus shot?
3. Why did the truck driver dump the load of loam on the wrong side of the house?
4. Was that the phone ringing?
5. Where the hell did I leave my shears?
6. Is that a *leak* in the new garden hose?
7. Didn't I have more tomato stakes last year?
8. Who put a soda can in the compost?
9. How did peat moss get inside my bra?
10. Are you sure that wasn't the phone?

WILD THING,
YOU MAKE MY HEART SING

I never tire of listening to Irene Stuckey describe her years as the only woman on the faculty of the University of Rhode Island's agriculture school. Besides her accomplishments as a researcher, wild plant expert and outspoken single working woman, the thing I really love about Irene is her voice.

After six decades among Yankees whose phrase when describing someone suffering cardiac arrest is "he took a hot" (that's *heart* to everyone south of Jersey), she has clung tenaciously to the gentle Georgia drawl of her home state.

So when she is talking about growing up the daughter of a renowned horticulturist—an associate of FDR and a man to whom scientists and academics from across the country turned with thorny problems—her voice is like honey being dribbled over trail mix. It's a combination of softness and raspiness, both overladen by old school gentility.

"I was an awkward child and my parents worked very hard so that I learned how to handle various situations," she says. "Eventually I learned a certain amount of diplomacy but I'm not one of these born-tactful people." Then she laughs and confesses, "I was only twenty-six when I came here in 1937 but I must have hit the place like a bombshell. If you're a scientist and you can be tactful, fine, but truth comes first."

As we say down South, where I, too, was born, she's not afraid to call a spade a shovel.

Irene Stuckey, retired as a professor of plant physiology in the School of Agriculture, has long been a legend, revered as an author and lecturer on wildflowers and honored for her vital research work.

While most people are content to observe nature from inside a car or in front of a television set, Irene needs to feel it under her feet, to reach out and pull apart petals and poke her nose inside to absorb the fragrance. (I was with her once when she pried open a skunk cabbage on a damp May morning. They aren't called skunk cabbage for nothing. "Wow!" I said, wrinkling my nose. "That's pungent."

"Yes, isn't it," she replied cheerfully, as though she'd just inhaled Chanel No. 5.)

Irene needs to see for herself where predatory plants are taking over and beautiful native species are being threatened, where birds have dropped seeds that caused things to sprout in unlikely places. Most importantly, she needs to pass along her passion for plants to others. She has been tracking where the wild things are for most of her eighty-five years without even a momentary lapse of enthusiasm. Despite the necessity of using a

DOWNY YELLOW VIOLET

cane since falling down the steps at home and breaking her ankle (two steel plates; fourteen screws) she has slowed remarkably little. She still walks woodland trails with sureness of foot, using the cane to point to plants or to hold aside branches that block the view.

She loves to show nature's incongruities such as tall blue-stem grass—thought of as prairie grass—that's found in the woods of western Rhode Island. And what of the *yellow* violets? People don't believe they're violets, she says, adding, "There are about five different white violets in Rhode Island; the flowers all look alike but the leaves are different."

As generations of initially reluctant university students have discovered, it's easy to get hooked on wildflowers once Dr. Stuckey has opened your eyes to the depth and intensity of the beauty that's all around. In fact, it is impossible to accompany her on one of her nature walks without wanting to know more.

To this end, she has a new book in the works. She has spent the last few summers traversing the Eastern Seaboard from Northern Massachusetts to Northern Florida and around to Louisiana cataloguing and photographing seaside plants for a forthcoming volume. It is the latest in a series of field guides that she's written and illustrated throughout her career. (Over the years all proceeds from her book sales and lecture and consulting fees went into a wildflower fund she established at the university.)

While she's known among her colleagues for her study of bent grass and her classic research on pasture renovation—during World War II she did her bit for the nation by showing how to efficiently raise forage crops for farm animals—to the public she's simply the Wildflower Lady. Her name has come to be synonymous with the spring walks through the nature preserve at the University of Rhode Island's W. Alton Jones campus.

No one knows the trails better because, after all, it was she who mapped them, in 1961.

The university had suddenly found itself in possession of a vast woodland where millionaire industrialist W. Alton Jones had kept a summer estate for fishing and hunting—and entertaining influential pals like President Eisenhower.

"I went over the whole twenty-three hundred acres foot by foot," says Irene, whose abiding love affair with this terrain endeared her to Nettie Marie Jones, the wealthy widow who gave the estate to the school. Sometimes Mrs. Jones would stroll with her.

"When she came here I used to be invited up to dinner. She was in her eighties by then, a very intelligent woman and thoroughly delightful."

The first summer that the university owned the land,

says Irene, "they told me to spend as much time as I could up there so I squeezed it in. My work was never official; my main work was research."

But she did such a fine job, made the nature preserve such a popular destination—her wildflower walks were always sold out weeks in advance—that during her final ten years on the faculty she was transferred to the Cooperative Extension Service so she could spend more time leading field trips. No one was more stunned than she by the response. One year, she says, "I had twelve hundred people for field trips. We had to schedule three a day."

When mapping the trails through an estate accumulated when the Joneses and the Louttits (the previous owners) had bought up failed farms, Stuckey followed old Indian trails and abandoned town roads. "I had hoped to make more new trails," she says, "but we didn't have the money. If you're taking people through the woods you've got to keep them on trails or they'll trample down your choice plants."

Irene Stuckey has been mesmerized by wildflowers all her life, a fascination inherited from her late father, the distinguished horticulturist Henry Perkins (H.P.) Stuckey, director of the Agriculture Experiment Station in Stuckey's native Georgia, one of only two such independent, non-university affiliated operations in the country. (Her family is, by the way, related to those other famous Stuckey's, the pecan pie purveyors whose shops are found at roadsides throughout the South. They're cousins.)

"My father wasn't the typical man of his generation," she explains. "He graduated from Clemson when it was a strict military school so he had that military attitude that you should be an officer and a gentleman but he also believed that women ought to be educated and they should be able to support themselves."

After Clemson, H.P. Stuckey went on to Cornell where he studied horticulture with Liberty Hyde Bailey and they became lifelong friends. A native South Carolinian, he returned there to teach horticulture at Winthrop College. Although, as his daughter points out, "Dad hated teaching and he didn't like Winthrop, so he only stayed a year," it was a year well spent. During his brief tenure he met his future wife, Cornelia Childress Martin, also a teacher, and descended from the early settlers of Nashville.

"Dad said she had the best mind of anybody he'd ever encountered," says Stuckey. "She had a masters from the University of Chicago and was planning to go to Harvard for a Ph.D. when I came along."

The family eventually would include three girls and a boy and Irene recalls her father preaching the value of education. "He said none of his daughters would ever marry for a meal ticket. He saw to it that all of us girls had educations as good as our brother had."

Known throughout the academic world for his research, H.P. Stuckey churned out reams of scientific treatises—another trait that his daughter would emulate later when she became a leading expert in the field of pasture grasses and was much in demand to present papers to learned societies.

"Dad was a prolific writer," she says. "We had one room that had papers stacked up against a wall with a brick on top of each pile and none of us was allowed to ever set foot inside. When I was in the baby carriage stage Dad used to take me out in the field with him so Mother could stay home and type and work on his manuscripts. He was doing plant breeding research on plums and he had me with him. He picked the first ones off and tucked them under the blanket of the baby carriage. When he went to examine them at noon he discovered that I had eaten the plums! They rushed me to the doctor because Dad was worried the plums would make me sick. Mother was upset because Dad had lost five years of research. I ate the plums—skin, seeds and all—and was not disturbed in the least!"

The young Irene so loved tagging around the fields and greenhouses with her father that when the time came to go to school she feigned illness in order to stay home.

"Mother had taught me first grade and I didn't want to go on to school at all: I'd much rather be with Dad. So Mother made a rule that if I said I was sick and couldn't go to school, then I had to stay in bed all day. That took care of that. But I spent as much time as I could out in the field with him because I enjoyed it so much. He would always explain to me what he was doing. My mother encouraged me to learn the Latin names because she taught Latin and English composition."

Sometimes Irene's enthusiasm for and pride in her father's work nearly overwhelmed her: She could recite reams of information about his projects and often did.

"Dad was the first to demonstrate in plants the marking character—that you could look at the color of the tendrils on seedling grapes when they had two leaves and two tendrils and if the tendrils were pale green, the fruit would be white; if they were rosy purple the fruit would be black."

Once when she was demonstrating to a friend how to predict the color of the fruit, her mother pulled her aside and said, "Irene, I know you're genuinely interested in this but not everyone is. Be careful that you don't appear to be showing off."

Irene likes to say that her father "knew all the best minds in the country from President Roosevelt down." (FDR, who spent a lot of time in Warm Springs, was, she recalls "a man who needed to have people around him and a lot of the local men would go see him. Dad and his friends used to see to it that someone would visit him every two to three days. The saying went that, during wartime, President Roosevelt was a lot safer in Warm Springs. It was all unmarked country roads and woods. If a stranger set foot across the county line everybody knew about it.")

After completing undergraduate work at Vanderbilt in chemistry, physics, and math, Irene Stuckey went to Cornell for a doctorate in plant physiology and cytology.

"Over the years if any of the Cornell professors wanted information on any of the plants of Georgia they'd write to Dad to make arrangements to get them." Usually the one doing the actual collecting of the samples in question was the young Irene.

"When I went to Cornell as a graduate student, at twenty-one, there was all this dithering back and forth. Liberty Hyde Bailey was ninety then and there was concern about his state of health: He was getting a little frail. But they wanted this class in taxonomy that I was in to go down and visit the hortatorium and meet him. They had one of those big old shingled houses, a fireproof brick hortatorium and a long fireproof corridor between them. One side of that corridor was all wide benches where you could lay out specimens in the window to work on them.

"We lined up along this long corridor and they brought Professor Bailey by and introduced him to each one. When he got to me he said, 'Oh, yes, my dear. I've been working today on some of the plants you collected for me.'

"I could see that my classmates were amazed. Professor Bailey had written a monograph on blackberries and I had spent a couple of summers collecting blackberry specimens. Oh, they're miserable things with all the thorns! They had to be collected with fruit on them, pressed and dried the way you do those things. The members of my class made a dive for all the blackberry specimens laid out and read the notice of the collector. I'd been about twelve when I collected them. Dr. Bailey was one of the international experts on plant anatomy. I knew all of those people by name long before I got to Cornell."

Another sign (albeit a rather amusing one) that young Irene was already on the fast track was her listing, while still a graduate student, in *American Men of Science*, the equivalent of *Who's Who*. It was her war-era research that really put her on the map and got her invited into another of the all-male clubs: the National Agronomy Society.

"I was invited to join because they were interested in

"[IRENE STUCKEY] HAS BEEN TRACKING
WHERE THE WILD THINGS ARE FOR MOST OF HER
EIGHTY-FIVE YEARS WITHOUT EVEN A MOMENTARY
LAPSE OF ENTHUSIASM."

the research I was doing and they asked me to come and give a paper. During the years I was active there were only three of us: Meta Brown, a cotton geneticist from Mississippi, Gertrude Cox who was THE famous statistician from North Carolina, and me. Now there are quite a few women in the agronomy society.

"I never ran into any prejudice except once. There was a Northeast summer meeting at Penn State. I'd come to Rhode Island to work on pastures. They'd had surveys and decided the big need for Northeast agriculture was to develop grazing for cattle so it would be cheaper to grow instead of feeding them hay and grain. So we worked on pastures and we really knew very little about pasture grasses. This Englishman at Cornell was pushing dwarf timothy. I did my own research and found that dwarfs didn't have the strength to compete; weeds came in vigorously. Dwarf bent grass didn't work and dwarf timothy was worse. It didn't grow. At the agronomy society meeting I got up and said, 'I've grown it and I didn't like it.' This Englishman made some scathing comment like, 'You can't believe anything a *woman* says.' The chairman of the meeting was furious. He took him apart in small pieces."

These days, as she obligingly takes guests on walks among the native chestnut and American beech, as she glories in the columbine and wild woodruff, Irene Stuckey is tremendously worried that, in general, people don't understand land management. All wild things aren't necessarily good; some are predators. And the biggest enemy of all is the commercial developer whose first act when preparing a building site is to go in and bulldoze everything in sight.

Making a rueful joke, she says, "I'm not sure there'll be any plants left by the time I get my book finished.

"The thing that bothers me is that people still don't understand about keeping land in its natural state, setting land aside to be undisturbed. Even the best-hearted people don't seem to have any understanding that land goes through stages of transition and it has to be managed. When people first got interested in ecology forty years ago this woman who had a Ph.D. from the University of Wisconsin and should have known better said something that made me hit the ceiling. When we received the nature preserve, she said, quite happily, 'Now you won't have to manage it; nature will take care of it.' It badly needed managing and now a lot of the rare things that were there originally are gone because they've been overwhelmed by other more vigorous plants. Invasive exotics have come in—bittersweet, multiflora rose, Japanese knotweed. Those are the worst: the hardest to get rid of and the first to come in. I was in Seattle and I wanted to call the mayor and say, 'Please dig up that multiflora rose on all the median strips.' People just don't understand these things. How can we teach them?"

One of the most active organizations in the state in terms of educating people about wildflowers and ecology is the Rhode Island Wild Plant Society of which Irene Stuckey is a founding member. The group offers lectures, slide shows, nature walks, and day trips to view the finest plant specimens in the region.

A rapt focus on her work kept Irene Stuckey from marrying although it was not for lack of opportunity. When it came to science versus men, however, it was no contest. With a hilarious directness that her mother would find appalling, she says, "I never knew any man whose face I wanted to see across the breakfast table every day."

Had she married, Dr. Stuckey might not have had time to become the legend that we in Rhode Island hold in such high esteem. Thousands of people who have taken her wildflower walks are quite selfishly glad that she wasn't home making someone's breakfast.

"I've enjoyed living in Rhode Island," she says. "People are much more tolerant and broadminded. Nobody ever questioned if I should do field work. Nobody ever interfered with my research. I'd plan it and do it and that was that. I had freedom to work as I pleased."

She traces her academic freedom to the early days of Rhode Island when sea captains and fabric manufacturers went off to make a living, confidently leaving everything at home in the control of their wives. The women, she says, "ran things on the same level as men and, to this very day, they have a lot more freedom of thought and activity."

So she likes to say that, when she came here in 1937 as the only woman in the agriculture department "nobody thought anything of it."

To the contrary: A great deal is thought of this tiny giant among the "men of science." I am personally grateful that she has helped me see with new eyes the most essential flower bed of all: Mother Nature's.

WHEN IRIS EYES
ARE SMILING

Long before it was a book and movie, the color purple was an iris; at least, I thought all irises were purple.

But then one day I brought my car to a screeching halt in front of Mini Manor Kennel because there were irises galore and only a few were purple. As other admirers whipped out their Sure Shots to grab a few snaps, I was stood on my ear by kennel owner Ed Anderson's rainbow of salmon, pink, bronze, lacy blue, and, yes, even black, blooms as glossy and seductive as a satin negligee.

In a curious way the splashy irises and the feathery miniature long-haired dachshunds he raises are reflections of Ed's personality. An elfin, silver-haired man who is a former championship ballroom dancer and career Air Force officer, he is fond of the flamboyant visual statement.

Blinded by his floral fireworks, I ordered two dozen color variations from Ed's supplier in Oregon. When they arrived I planted them in a raised bed, specially built for the occasion. The soil was dark and rich, and I made it even richer by adding a quantity of odiferous cow manure.

To create a pleasing mixture of height and texture, I located the rhizomes among other flowers, including miniature roses and baby's breath. Next I poured on more fertilizer. I treated the bed to a nightly drenching.

Although I didn't actually say aloud, "I shall be the envy of the neighborhood!" I thought it.

After two weeks I noticed only a few limp green blades had emerged. I went back to Ed to report my new irises were very unhappy campers.

"Irises don't like to be interplanted with other flowers," he told me. "They hate competition."

"Oh," I said.

"And they don't like to be heavily fertilized. Actually they prefer a relatively poor soil."

"Oh," I said.

"Also, you mustn't overwater. It causes disease."

"Oh," I said.

In a matter of minutes, I went from imagining myself the star of *The Victory Garden* to feeling like the Lucretia Borgia of the plant world. This happens when a greenhorn has had a few early successes. Mother Nature is always lurking, waiting to give you your comeuppance.

Ed's style of gardening is calm and disciplined. He's precisely the sort of grower you'd expect a military man to be. In his typically methodical manner he chooses his flowers and forms his beds systematically. His discovery of irises turned out to be his crowning achievement.

IRISES: 1 POGON, 2 ONOCYCLUS, 3 EVANSIA,
4 APOGON, 5 SIBERIAN, 6 JAPANESE,
7 RHIZOME, 8 BULB

In one fell swoop he found a flower that suited his love of the elegant statement while, at the same time, required little care.

He got hooked on irises while mapping out a beautification project for his eight-acre kennel property. He built a cobblestone pond fed by a gurgling waterfall, planted flowering azalea and rhododendron along the edges of his woodland, and carved out a homey, comfortable patio space surrounded by spring bulbs.

Then he began considering an elevated area along his driveway for a flowerbed, trying to decide what would do well in sandy, well-drained soil with full sun exposure. And, because he's busy overseeing as many as eighty visiting pets at any given time, he wanted a variety of flower that wouldn't demand a lot of fussing.

"I saw an article about irises—and, honestly, it was never a flower I'd thought about—and said, 'This is something I've got to do some day,'" he told me. "It doesn't really hold well if you cut it for an arrangement and I didn't think the iris had a very long blooming life. I figured a day or two and the blossoms would be all gone and that would be it."

Nonetheless, he sent in two dollars for the catalogue and, when it arrived, all his misconceptions evaporated. "I was most surprised at the variety, the shapes, colors, and sizes they were talking about. I never knew all this existed! I was concerned they'd only bloom a brief time, but I decided to go ahead and try them anyway."

Having a natural flair for color as well as a tendency to be meticulous, he chose shadings that would embrace each other and made a list of what he had ordered and how he planned to arrange them. After he sent in his order, he did what I should have done—homework.

"The first and most important thing I did was to take a soil sample to the university's agricultural extension service. I told them I planned to grow irises and asked them what I needed to do," he recalled.

(*Now* you tell me, I thought, lamenting that I hadn't asked before it was too late.)

"They gave me a breakdown of my soil, which turned out to be silt-sand-loam, which was almost perfect." (As opposed to my own dark, heavy soil, which was just about the kiss of death.)

When the flowers arrived, Ed put them in with numbered stakes and figured he wouldn't see much in the way of results for at least two years.

"Spring came and all hell broke loose! I had the most beautiful display of irises, and I'd really done very little. And they bloomed for three to four weeks with as many as four or five blooms on each stem!"

Between the irises he planted grape hyacinths, which bloom first and then die back, allowing the irises to wave above them. When the irises have finished blooming, he's content to have their bright green stalks form a background for his annuals.

Ed Anderson's intense interest in flowers melded with his love of animals when he was stationed in England at the end of his Air Force service. By the time he retired as master sergeant, he'd put in twenty-one years—far longer than he'd ever intended to stay. Early on, he'd set his sights on becoming a florist.

"I majored in agriculture in high school, and I had to choose a project for three years," he said. "Some of the boys raised cattle and others worked with different vegetable crops; I cultivated chrysanthemums. At the same time, I worked in a greenhouse doing spring planting."

After graduation he attended a junior college affiliated with Clemson University, where his horticultural career got short-circuited. A prize-winning ballroom dancer, he was soon pressed into organizing sessions of fox-trots, waltzes, and rhumbas for students, faculty, and townspeople.

Short and trim, Ed is extremely quick on his feet, wasting little time and displaying a penchant for using his small, graceful hands to gesture as he speaks. With his twinkly smile, cheerful personality, and well-groomed Perry Como good looks, he was much in demand at Clemson.

The administration was so delighted with the success

of his wholesome, well-attended dance classes that one or two nights turned into five. Ed's studies went down the drain.

Meanwhile, Uncle Sam was waiting to put *his* name on Ed's dance card.

"I had the draft hanging over me, so I enlisted to get my military obligation out of the way. To my surprise, I found a home in the military. I got put into the recreation and entertainment section and wound up running golf courses, bowling alleys, and recreation centers all over the world."

But he also kept his hand in with gardening, finding the tour of duty in England in the mid-1970s perfect for the hobby.

"When I was advanced far enough in rank to have my own home and not be living in the barracks, I always had a garden, and the nicest I ever had was in England. There you can just throw a seed and it blooms and blooms. You can raise anything over there because the climate is perfect—mild winters and cool summers. I had twenty-eight rose varieties, some as tall as my house. One of the things that impressed me so in England was how much everyone is into flowers—even people who have tiny yards with a door and a little fenced-in area divided by a walkway will have 150 flowers blooming. Everything is perfectly manicured because they go out and spend an hour every morning in the garden."

When Ed returned to America and retired, he brought with him two things: a desire to continue growing things and a fluffy miniature long-haired dachshund who would become the grande dame of what is now a sort of mini-dynasty of championship dogs.

Settling into his present location in 1980, he began cultivating flowers and puppies with a passion. Soon his garden was thriving, as were his kennel business and his reputation for breeding Best of Show dogs which attract buyers from across the country.

"The ordinary," he declares, "doesn't turn me on. I always want to do things that are a little different. I don't think it's in bad taste, but I *do* tend to lean a little toward the more extravagant. Where some men don't like to wear a bright red tie, I probably would. It's the same with the iris colors I go through. There are many flowers I don't grow because they're ordinary and uninteresting. The flowers I select are ones that make me go 'Oh, wow!' and it's also true of the dachshunds. Most people see them and say, 'Oh, wow!'

"I've got dogs that stop traffic and flowers that stop traffic, and that gives me pleasure—to see people enjoy something I've done or selected."

As an expert in both, Ed Anderson believes you can tell a lot about people by their gardens and their pets.

"People who adopt mixed-breed dogs from the pound grow wildflowers. People who like unusual dogs prefer exotic flowers. But you have to set limits on yourself." (In other words: You couldn't keep an Old English sheepdog in an efficiency apartment and palm trees don't grow in Alaska.)

Ed's original iris plants wound up creating hundreds of babies, so the parent plants had to be dug up and the off-shoots cut apart.

"You have to be sure you get under the root so the rhizome lies on top," he explains. "You discard the one that bloomed last year and keep the rest. When I cut them up some had five or six new rhizomes and one actually had thirty new starter plants. I was pointing and telling a helper where to plant them and, pretty soon, I didn't know what had gone where. Now I'll have to wait until they bloom so I can identify and tag them."

His dogs, meanwhile, have descended from the little English immigrant named Shotzie (who lived to be nearly twenty) to become champions in every major show ring. One named Blue Max was the first miniature long-haired dachshund ever to win the top prize of the Dachshund Club of America, defeating 400 others.

In the past five years, Ed has made converts—or at least those who dare to dream—out of practically everyone who comes to buy a puppy or board a pet. People come away loving the sweet little dogs which resemble furry bedroom slippers and admiring the velvet-plumed irises.

"They see the show the irises put on and they all want to borrow the catalogue," Ed says, laughing. "I feel like the library: The minute the book comes back, somebody else is on the list to take it out."

And then, of course, some of us ought to be fined for not paying closer attention to the rules.

Even though I don't seem to have much of a hand for irises—or for controlling bossy little dogs, for that matter—I still admire Ed's natural control of animals and plants. I wish I were less of a wimp at doggie discipline, and had different soil or better sense.

Having looked hungrily at his irises in brilliant cry— the saber-shaped peach blossoms with burgundy throats, the delft blue beauties with the touch of lemon—and having desperately wanted to have a rousing success with a variety named Martha Mia!, I've had to concede that it's not in the cards.

Although it was demoralizing, my iris debacle wasn't a financial or physical tragedy. Other gardening failures, on the other hand, have allowed me to redefine back pain and muscle ache—not to mention the jolt to the checkbook for medical and pharmaceutical bills— largely because I lack the willpower necessary to Just Say No to certain flowers I'm tempted to try.

Some flowers, I'm here to testify, can be harmful to your health. Take my canna lilies, for instance. Please.

PERSONALITY TYPES AND THEIR FAVORITE PLANTS AND PETS: A MATCH-UP LIST

Personality Type	Plant, Pet Preference
Tall blonde with perfect posture and a dazzling smile	Sunflowers; golden retriever
High-powered, short-tempered executive with no time, a FAX machine, and a BMW with a car phone	Prickly Pear and cactus, surrounded by an electric fence; Doberman
TV evangelist	Jack-in-the pulpit, money-plant, glory lilies; snow white dove
Pacifist clerking in a health-food store	Organic herb garden heavy on catnip, bed of Peace roses; seventeen adopted stray cats.
Detroit auto executive trying to figure out how to beat foreign imports	Japanese meditation garden; piranha
Construction magnate with a resume full of skyscrapers and mansions	A rock garden and a rottweiler
Drug dealer	Marijuana, poppies, and a pit bull

Personality Type	Plant, Pet Preference
Former debutante, Mayflower descendant, socialite, winter resident of Palm Beach, Republican	Formal English garden with a caretaker; King Charles spaniel
Cop	Perennial garden, carefully fenced; German shepherd
Nun	Madonna's cloak, a shrine in a bathtub; long-haired black cat with a white bib and paws
CIA agent	Secret garden; bloodhound
Jazz musician	Trumpet lilies, cymbal plant; cool cat
Controversial talk show host	Two-lips, gum trees; parrot
Exterminator	Venus flytrap, spider plant; anteater
Elderly person with memory lapses	Forget-me-nots; an elephant
House painter	Jacob's ladder; a horse named Old Paint
Delivery boy in a rainy climate	Japanese umbrella pine; water spaniel

Personality Type	Plant, Pet Preference
Burglar	Mask flower; raccoon
Physician	Syringa plant; porcupine
Bartender	Brewer's Weeping Spruce, barley crop; St. Bernard
A person who has undergone a face-lift, a nose job, liposuction, and a tummy tuck	Plastic plants and a stuffed dog
Strong-willed, frenetic writer with too much energy and a tendency toward sassiness	Fuss-budget garden full of impatiens, troublesome dahlias; equally sassy smooth-haired fox terrier

CANNA LILY
KILL YA?

The canna lilies seemed harmless when they were given to me by a friend who was dividing his crop after winter storage. Admittedly, the clumps of tubers clustered together like so many giant yams *did* seem unwieldy, but I was assured that if I divided the root system into three plantings, I'd have an entire row of tall, exotic-looking plants with huge green foliage topped by scarlet plumes.

I had never grown canna lilies, but I was game for something new. I lugged the starter sets to the widest end of my garden and began digging holes. First I'd dig, then I'd try to fit one in, then I'd dig some more. I began to think I was likely to hit China before I'd made a space large enough to accommodate them.

Ultimately I succeeded with the first, and then, several bucketsful of dirt later, I had made two more cavernous trenches. It took nearly an hour to get these flowers planted. At the time, it seemed excessive, but because it's not polite to complain about free flowers, I finished the job and then went searching for the heating pad.

As weeks passed and nearby dahlias started pushing through the ground, I began to wonder where the cannas were. Eventually green furled leaves resembling hand-rolled cigars sprouted from one plant site, but there was no sign of its companions.

"How can this be?" I asked a visiting gardener pal. "They were all planted at the same time, in the same soil, under precisely the same conditions. What happened to the other two?"

"Well, maybe you planted them too deep," he suggested, probing the ground with his finger. When nothing turned up, he got a stick and started poking around.

"Are you sure this is where you put them?" he asked, as though I could forget such an event. When I assured him there could be no mistake, he began to dig in earnest with his hands, like a large dog looking for the steak bone he buried the previous summer. His efforts were to no avail; there was no sign of the missing cannas. I wrote the whole thing off to them having fallen victim to some mysterious deadly illness, and planted more dahlias where they'd been.

And then, of course, they came up, elbowing their way into the dahlia rows and shoving everything aside, like sailors on shore leave bellying up to a crowded bar. These were not flowers, they were volcanoes. The dahlias struggled to maintain their foothold but with little success. They grew with crooked stalks, leaning at a crazy angle pitched away from the greedy enormity of the cannas. Their blossoms were small and self-conscious; they had almost no foliage.

CANNA LILIES

The cannas were unrepentant, growing ever taller, spreading their huge leafy arms wider and wider until I was forced to walk in a Groucho Marx crouch in order to get near enough to do basic weeding. Under the soil, I would later learn in a painful botanical lesson, things were even more dramatic: In order to support the six-foot-tall stalks, the canna root system was expanding, storing up nutrients in an explosion of massive tubers.

It occurred to me that I had the makings of a Stephen King novel in my garden. Perhaps I could call it *The Canna Lily That Came to Kill*. The movie rights would be sold for millions, and people would flock to theaters, paying large amounts for the privilege of being scared silly by my ferocious flora.

There is an entire film history of vengeful plants devouring their unsuspecting owners—cute little flowers that turn into gigantic mutants who polish off Cleveland for lunch. After watching the canna grow even larger and more intimidating, I began to fantasize. The results were frightening.

Send Me No Flowers. A woman with a plant phobia is murdered by an exploding florist's box.

Conan the Agrarian. A maniacal botanist with large muscles conquers the world by creating an army of lethal perennials.

Demon Seed. The Prince of Darkness infiltrates the

garden of a monastery by posing as a hybrid monk's hood.

The Blob. A cherry tomato plant goes berserk and smears red goo everywhere, turning a whole town into scarlet mush.

The Thing. An obscure and frail vegetable plant, purchased for a dime at a yard sale, grows into a 700-pound squash, crushing to death the little old lady who merely wanted to give it a nice home.

Children of the Corn. Aliens invade a corn crop, turning the baby ears into killer cobs that bludgeon villagers to death.

The Dark Secret of Harvest Home. Mild-mannered Farmer Jones has no idea that his threshing machine plans to mow him down instead of the wheat.

Eaten Alive. A woman reaches out to munch a pea pod fresh from the vine and is, instead, dragged screaming into the bushes where she herself becomes fresh lunch—Gardener Tartare.

The House That Dripped Blood. A climbing rose escapes its trellis by night, invading a house and pricking an entire family to death with its thorns.

The Incredible Two-Headed Transplant. An Iowa gardener experiments by crossing a Deadly Nightshade with a Daylily, only to find himself sliced and diced by his own creation—The Deadly Night and Day Lily Shade.

Make Them Die Slowly. Neglected houseplants revolt

against the woman who went on vacation, forgetting to water them. They stick her in a small, hot bucket of dry dirt, shine ultraviolet lights on her, and refuse to give her a drink until she eventually goes mad.

Monster from Green Hell. Bibb lettuce grown on a city terrace organizes other patio vegetables to take over their apartment building in Brooklyn, demanding protection money from the human tenants.

World Gone Wild. A woman fails to tend her garden properly and the weeds take over, eventually spreading to the nation's capital and capturing the White House Rose Garden.

I knew that my gargantuan canna lilies had the power—and possibly the desire—to do something similar, but would they? I adopted a wait-and-see attitude.

By midsummer their scarlet flowers, like so many ruffled topknots, were shooting from the center of the greenery and attracting Japanese beetles—who seemed to like their color—from miles around. Once they were happily ensconced in my garden, the bugs lived among the canna leaves, using them as home base for foraging attacks on nearby rose bushes. Tender pink buds would be munched from the inside out, totally riddled with holes before they even had a chance to open. Every time I looked at the cannas, waving like so many banners in front of an auto dealership, I seethed.

Nonetheless, it was their overendowed grandeur that

drew the most praise from passersby, who would invariably stop to get a closer look at the beds. They would almost always gloss over the dahlias and roses in order to swoon before the cannas.

"Aren't they spectacular!" said one woman, noting she'd love to have some when I dug them up.

I resisted the urge to tell her she could have the whole damn lot of them because I knew it would take a forklift to hoist them up and cart them away.

"How dramatic!" sighed her companion. "They remind me of paradise vacation spots; you know, those places with all the lovely tropical flowers."

The cannas reminded me of a tropical place, too: Hell.

They were a nuisance, an annoyance, a pest collection center, an example of something out of sync and scale with its surroundings. They were like a grand piano in a galley kitchen—simply too much.

When fall came and it was time to bring in the nonhardy tubers, I remembered all the people who'd admired the cannas and thought about how generosity is one of the endearing traits of a happy gardener. Even though I'd come to loathe the cannas' treelike brazenness, there were others who had asked for starter plants from my cannas the following spring. Based on how they'd grown and spread, I figured digging up one plant for winter storage would provide a sufficient number of bulbs to give away.

One broken shovel handle, one shattered wheelbarrow axle, and three trips to the chiropractor later, I realized that it is *not* always more blessed to give than to receive. Each of the cannas had sprouted dozens of heavy, interconnected bulbs. Trying to dig under a single root system took an entire morning and made me seriously consider buying blasting caps. After the plant was freed from the ground by my personal version of a leveraged digout—I used two shovels positioned on opposite sides of the godawful root—I remembered that some poor slob would have to lift the thing into the wheelbarrow.

Me.

After a summer spent working daily at fairly rigorous garden chores, I didn't consider myself out of shape, but trying to lift the horrendously heavy canna lily was like bench-pressing a Chrysler.

"Where's Arnold Schwarzenegger when I need him?" I moaned, staggering under what was easily a sixty-pound load, and one that I'd only gotten about knee-high. I knew it was a mistake to try hobbling with it in that position but I saw no alternative.

After I'd made the agonizing trip (approximately three yards) to the wheelbarrow, I discovered I was unable to lift my burden high enough to load it, so I tried tilting the wheelbarrow nose down in hopes of rolling the thing in. It worked; the killer canna did roll in, but returning the wheelbarrow to an upright position was another matter. That's how the axle broke; it snapped right off like a toothpick trying to support a cement block.

You'd think by now I would've learned my lesson but, somehow, the series of tortuous events only made me more determined to finish the job. I was so furious that I didn't care if the neighbors found my body under the twisted wreckage of the wheelbarrow, shovels, and plant roots. I was not going to be bested by a plant that I'd never even liked in the first place.

Scouring through my storage room, the sort of jumble collection that flea market aficionados would appreciate, I found a large cardboard box once used to house a new microwave oven. I returned to the garden and dumped the canna from the wheelbarrow into the box. Then, assuming the bent-over position that helps orthopedists buy condominiums in Acapulco, I began crawling backward, dragging the box toward my car.

Twenty minutes later, I was using my last ounce of energy to curse and cajole the canna up off the ground and into the trunk. There is nothing in Olympic weight-lifting competition that even approaches the challenge of a short, exhausted woman straining to raise sixty pounds of roots in a sagging box.

Somehow I managed it and drove to the end of the street where a neighbor who'd coveted the cannas had volunteered to store the massive tubers in his garage, in exchange for my promise to divide and plant them in the spring—in his yard. It seemed like a good deal to me.

He helped me unload the thing, and we stashed it under a stairway. I went home and collapsed, arising only to call for an appointment at the nearest spine-adjustment clinic.

When I showed up for the appointment—manipulation, it's called—I was a misshapen mess, barely able to sit or stand without whimpering pathetically.

"What happened to you?" asked the perky young man in the white coat.

"I've been gardening," I said.

"I'll bet you were lifting something improperly," he said with a Sherlock Holmes tone of superiority. "I suppose you just bent over and put the entire strain on your back. People never remember to bend their knees and squat beside the object they're lifting."

If I could've raised my arm, let alone squatted, I would have cheerfully wiped the smug look off his face.

"Ever try lifting the Canna Lily That Ate Cleveland?" I asked.

"Ah," he smiled, as he led me to a table and began wrenching my arms and legs in various anatomically improbable positions. "I see a lot of gardeners. You people always seem to bite off more than you can chew. Didn't anyone ever tell you that it's better to do things in moderation?"

"No," I replied, from between clenched teeth. "I had a very poor role model. My mother used to carry the living room sofa around the house by herself when she was in one of her furniture-moving moods."

The chiropractor continued pummeling me. At the end of the session, once the pain of the treatment stopped, I felt much better. He prescribed a second visit and handed me a brochure about lifting that I noticed covered such things as books, parcels, and infants but made no mention of items with which I normally wrestle: bales of hay, forty-pound bags of humus, peat moss that comes in five-cubic-yard containers, plant tubers the size of Third World nations.

By spring, my back had returned to normal and I no longer walked like an ape. On a warm day I wandered down to my neighbor's garage and peered into the box containing the cannas, which we'd stashed under the stairwell. They had rotted, having frozen during a mid-winter cold snap. When I pulled the box out, it was lighter than air.

My neighbor was disappointed but not devastated by the loss, but then, of course, he wasn't the one who nearly died trying to save it.

Canna lily kill ya? Yes, but only if you plant one in the first place.

The lesson here is that not all floral gifts should be accepted. Some are accidents waiting to happen while others are merely disagreeable. Cannas, in my opinion, are both. What a deal.

A FINE JOB FOR A WOMAN

W hen I drop in on Julie Morris she has spent the better part—if you can call it that—of a hot, humid July day pruning shrubs at Blithewold,* the turn-of-the-century seaside mansion where she has been a staff member for eighteen years and chief horticulturist for thirteen years.

She smiles and puts her usually placid spin on the arduous task: "Well," she says, "there's something very zen-like about pruning. You just do it and go on automatic pilot and it's actually rather restful."

I suppose she has to have this sort of resilience and work ethic since, after all, she does come to work every single day of the week. She doesn't necessarily stay all day and do a lot of things on a Sunday, for instance, but she checks in nonetheless to make sure that all is as it should be on the thirty-three acres that are her domain. So devoted is she to her duties that she gave up a nice home in Newport and moved to Bristol, where

---

*The original owner of Blithewold, completed in 1908, was Augustus van Wickle. His elder daughter, Marjorie van Wickle Lyon, inherited the house and, when she died at the age of 93, in 1976, she left it to the Heritage Trust of Rhode Island which owns a number of other prominent early homes.

Blithewold is located, so she'd be sure of getting to work each day no matter the weather.

"It *is* a seven day a week job," she says. "The greenhouse doesn't know when it's Saturday and Sunday." If Julie's out of town or too tuckered to drop by, her assistant, Gail Read, spells her.

The three high pressure times of year for the staff of Blithwolde, whose mansion and grounds are open to the public, are late winter (the Rhode Island Flower Show), spring, when a massive fundraising plant show is held, and the summer tourist season.

Incredibly, from a tiny greenhouse whose ceiling panels have been known to fall without warning, requiring heavy plastic sheeting to be wrapped overhead, Morris and her crew of Read and some thirty volunteers, turn out 18,000 annuals for the spring sale. "Our variety of annuals [including antique pansies in soft shades of rose and cream, sixteen kinds of salvia, vanilla-scented heliotrope, and old-fashioned sweet peas] is our claim to fame," says Julie. "They're unusual things that you can't just go to a nursery and pick up."

During the week before the plant sale—the horticultural equivalent of a fraternity's hell week—the greenhouse is filled with three tiers of flats covered with plastic. More flats are jammed into the potting shed and, even then, it's not enough space to contain the bounty so, inevitably, things have to be put outside under makeshift

"I've always been very happy growing
things in pots." —Julia Morris

lean-tos. Julie knows she's done her job well, though, on the morning of the plant sale when, the minute the doors are open, savvy gardeners charge in like pioneers answering the starting pistol for the California gold rush.

Just as Irene Stuckey was tremendously influenced by a man—her father—in the pursuit of a lifelong interest in plants, Julie Morris traces her passion for horticulture straight to her grandmother. "Her garden in Pennsylvania was the beginning. She was really a vegetable gardener but she gave me the first plants that I grew inside. I was eight or nine; it was the late 1940s and I kept those ivies for years. My first love is container-grown plants. I had a container garden in Philadelphia. I've always been very happy growing things in pots."

When her plans to attend Sarah Lawrence College got derailed, Julie turned to her grandmother for advice and that advice was: horticulture. "It was a great alternative," she says. She enrolled in a two-year program at the Pennsylvania School of Horticulture for Women which was, at the time, becoming part of Temple University. It had been started in 1917 by Elizabeth Lee, who was a landscape architect in a time when not many women were pursuing careers in that field.

"She wanted to start a school for 'genteel women of limited means who had to work,'" Julie explains. "In England gardening was an acceptable profession for women; there were many estates run by women in England."

Based on an English school, the Philadelphia operation was very practical. In the meantime, Temple wanted the property but part of the deal was that they had to keep the School of Horticulture. They not only abided by that proviso, they added to it. The study of horticulture is now a four-year degree program. Although Julie Morris went on to get a bachelor's degree in sociology, her heart was always in growing and, once again, her major influences were women.

"I was very lucky in the course of my career to know four really quite remarkable women who helped me at various stages," she says. "The first was Emily Cheston, who was an old family friend. At the time that I knew her, she was seventy and I was twenty and we were the best of friends until she died at the age of ninety-five. She gave me a job working in her garden which was very near the School of Horticulture. She was also a collector of old gardening books and that introduced me to a whole other world."

After Julie had graduated from horticultural school she met the second influential woman: Ernesta Ballard, author of a book called *Garden in Your House*, a best seller houseplant book in the late 1950s. "I worked in her greenhouses. She went on to become director of the Pennsylvania Horticultural Society and revitalized the

Philadelphia Flower Show. It exists in its present state because of Ernesta."

After working privately for Ernesta Ballard for five years, Julie made the move with her employer to the Pennsylvania Horticultural Society, where she stayed for seven years. "It was a wonderful experience," she recalls, "because Ernesta was very anxious that we all try our wings and be allowed to try new projects. She built the horticultural society up from a budget of $50,000 to one million by the time she left. She picked the Philadelphia Flower Show up and turned it into what it is now. We had the chance to meet horticulturists all over the country and I still have those ties. It's all as a result of my early days, going to meetings."

During her tenure with the horticultural society, Julie also worked in its enormous library where she met Elisabeth Woodburn, an antiquarian book dealer. "Betty Woodburn was a mentor in every way. She was also a very fine librarian. The Society library was second only to the Massachusetts Horticultural Society Library and is the oldest such library in the country." Another influence was Jean Byrne, editor of the *Green Scene* magazine who, says Julie, gave her confidence in her writing and encouraged her to submit pieces that were published.

As much as she had learned in Pennsylvania, Julie Morris began to miss her home state, Rhode Island, and twenty years ago she moved back which was a lucky thing for Blithewold and for all of us who have enjoyed the beautiful results of her handiwork. After running her own garden design and maintenance business for awhile ("I wasn't tough enough"), Julie began volunteering at Blithewold. She worked on the first newsletters and helped organize the friends' association. "Then we got a grant to have the trees identified and that was the first thing I did here. Over the course of two winters I identified the woody plant collection." (That collection, by the way, contains an exotic bamboo forest and an eighty-three foot giant Sequoia.)

Missing public horticulture, she signed on part-time and soon was the fulltime horticulturist responsible for the vast perennial gardens, the water and rock gardens, the breathtaking show of thousands of spring bulbs cascading across the lawn and down to the sea, the acres of trees also endangered by natural threats such as hurricanes and blizzards, and, of course, the production of the greenhouse.

Under her leadership the garden volunteer program was established—"We couldn't do what we do without them"—and the spring plant sale was built from a venture that took in a few hundred dollars to the blockbuster of 1996 that made $28,000. Meanwhile, Julie has led Blithewold to the forefront as a regional learning center. It was the site of a highly successful conference on management of historic landscapes attended by pro-

Miniature dahlias with
veronica, daylilies, phlox, and astilbe

fessionals and interested amateurs from the East coast as well as curators and preservationists.

For my part, I don't know how she keeps on top of it all. If I had to worry about replacing the eighty trees lost to Hurricane Bob or put up with tourists asking questions that could have inspired the film *Dumb and Dumber*, I would probably climb up the giant Sequoia and throw myself off.

Yet Julie Morris is unflappable. She is incredibly knowledgeable, hard-working, and accomplished. She's got an inordinate amount of patience. She does, however, confess that sometimes she feels the goldfish bowl effect of managing a public garden.

"I think there is a certain amount of pressure," she says. "It's not bad pressure, though. One of the sad things for me is that even when the garden looks absolutely wonderful—at the end of the day or when the colors really show, and I know it looks great—I'll walk around with people and all I'm likely to see is what needs to be done. That's what happens in your own garden. I go other places and I don't see the weeds because I don't need to. Every gardener I know who works in gardens that the public visits feels the same way. There are some marvelous private gardens around here and I think, '*How* do they do it?' Well, they're a little bit smaller; they can devote themselves to one garden. We have thirty-three acres here and there isn't any part of the property that doesn't need some work and rejuvenation. I have the feeling that we're always behind."

She's currently dealing with how to replace the lost trees, noting that the new school says that, instead of planting a single $500 tree, you plant ten fifty-dollar trees and wait for them to catch up.

She also frets about the difficulty of keeping things labeled. "We really need to keep up," she says. "Sometimes I feel impatient with visitors' questions but I realize that the American people really don't have the kind of cultural heritage about gardening that the English have. When I'm in England and hear a four-year-old say, "Oh, mummy, look at the *taxus cuspidata* [that's Japanese yew to the rest of us poor schlubs] I realize that just doesn't happen here. But people really *do* want to learn. I do like teaching.

"On Sundays people are here at a more leisurely pace. That's when it's really fun to talk to people in the garden, especially when they're on their own and not in a group. We have an emergency room doctor who lives not far away and has his own garden and five children. He comes here every week to poke around and ask questions. It's a very peaceful place. It's hard to get riled up."

Blithewold is unusual among the mansions open to the public because of its gardens. The Newport palaces

". . .BLANKETED WITH THOUSANDS OF DAFFODILS."

such as The Breakers and Marble House had cutting gardens that were located far away from the house. There was a small teahouse garden at Chateau-sur-Mer, a little rose garden at Rosecliff, and a sunken garden on the shadowy grounds of The Elms, but Blithewold alone, up the road in Bristol, offers the complete package. Soon, says Julie, it will be possible for garden lovers who've already taken the mansion tour to buy a grounds pass and enjoy the gardens while skipping the rest.

For fifteen years the North garden has been a palette of blue-and-yellow, the favorite colors of a late board member. The western side of the house, looking out over the bay, is a forest that, in spring, is blanketed with thousands of daffodils.

The cutting gardens near the greenhouse are filled with the type of perennial display that makes my mouth water. Julie and her helper, Gail, have laid them out in geometric patterns and raised areas instead of the more conventional (in my case, duller) horizontal rows. And here and there you find the unexpected.

"We don't use any chemical controls except on the driveway," explains Julie, "because I like seeing what might come up and there are always surprises. We make our own compost by shredding what comes out of the garden and putting it back on the gardens a year later.

It's very interesting to see the things that have seeded themselves."

Unlike Gail, whose favorite season is spring because starting seeds is the most exciting thing for her, Julie prefers autumn. "It's a little bit of a peaceful time here before we have to think about Christmas and the flower show. Things have calmed down in the garden. It's a time of year when I can take stock of what we've done and really enjoy the property. I like the way the light is, the longer shadows. The light is softer in the garden, the play of shadow and light. There are a lot of colors in the perennials—not in the flowers but the foliage. The conventional wisdom has always been that you clean everything up. We cut back the North garden but not the rock garden. We leave plants pretty much as they are; it helps protect them over the winter.

"The grasses of course are beautiful. We have dahlias around the pond that change colors and become more apricot each day."

Not normally a political animal, Julie Morris found herself offended enough to join with another woman to found Greenwimmen in response to the Boston Horticulture Club which did not allow women. In 1996 the organization changed its policy. "They asked if I wanted to be one of the first women members and actually I don't."

Her next major project looms ahead: The Blithewold

board plans to launch a one million dollar fundraising appeal to restore the historic greenhouse with curved-eave palm house and conservatory that was taken down in the 1930s and put in storage. All the pieces remain intact.

"That would be a great old-age job," she says, smiling. "Washing the windows and taking care of the display in the greenhouse."

Other than that, says Julie Morris, she does not expect to retire. "I plan to just plop over into the compost pile. They can leave me there."

MRS. GOODWIN,
WHO PLANTS MARIGOLDS
IN TRAFFIC ISLANDS

As my experience with the cannas demonstrates, one of the most indispensable tools in the amateur gardener's collection is a sense of humor.

You couldn't find a better example of someone who saw the fun in gardening—and, for that matter, a general delight with life—than Antoinetta Goodwin. I have to confess that Mrs. Goodwin—nobody my age would have *dared* to make so bold as to call her Etta, as did her contemporaries—had been one of my idols for nearly twenty years.

The first time I ever saw her, she was planting marigolds in the middle of a traffic island. She was wearing her usual uniform—dungarees, workshirt, boots—and crawling around on her hands and knees, digging, setting in plants, patting soil into place. She peered at me from under a huge straw hat as I stopped to admire her handiwork.

It was hard to miss Mrs. Goodwin when she was pursuing her private beautification program and that's because her car gave her away. It had two enormous plastic chickens, wearing matching sets of clothes and waving American flags, bolted to the roof rack.

I took one look at this elderly woman and her car and

said to myself, "I want to be just like that when I grow up." I was twenty-eight at the time.

Antoinetta Goodwin knew how to have fun. She was famous for her chickens (a smaller pair sat atop the mailbox in front of the farm where she raised Christmas trees), and for her pro bono flower planting.

The chickens were a patriotic salute to the Rhode Island Red, our state bird, but her own declaration of civic pride—the planting of flowers in public places—symbolized Mrs. Goodwin's desire to give something back in gratitude to the adopted country where her Italian immigrant parents found the good life they'd dreamed of.

Antoinetta Goodwin, born in America, was someone who found goodness and beauty everywhere and, if it didn't exist, she created it. That's what kept her young and feisty all her life.

To those who've followed her exploits through the years, she was a charming eccentric, a hands-on activist who took to heart the tenets of free expression and the pursuit of happiness. She was a perpetual political candidate, an Independent who ran alone on what she called the Rhode Island Red ticket. Indeed, with the passing of time, Mrs. Goodwin came to resemble her chickens—from her feathery puffs of gray hair and her small bright eyes peering down a sharp beaklike nose, right to the tasseled hats she knit for the chickens and herself.

When she scolded local officials for failing to do their jobs, her precise, high-pitched voice sounded remarkably like clucking.

She sometimes clucked about people's carelessness in stomping through the flowerbeds she planted in the center of crosswalks but, on the whole, gardening brought her great joy.

"I guess my inspiration for gardening came from a prominent local family who owned the textile mills," she once reflected. "They had a beautiful estate, right in the center of the village, and the kindergarten I attended was actually located on a corner of their property. As I walked to school, all I could see were lovely blooms—rhododendrons, azaleas, flowers of every kind growing along a picket fence. This family also provided land for the millworkers to have their own gardens and, as kids, we would take our baskets and help.

"During my teenage years, my mother did the gardening because I was too busy being young. But when I went to work as a beautician, I bought a house and began to plant."

In no time at all, she was beautifying the town as well as its women.

When she bought her first house, at a major intersection downtown, she operated a beauty parlor at the front, and she and her mother used the rest of the house to live in. They both set to work planting in the yard.

"Being Italian, my mother grew her tomatoes, peppers, and parsley, but I wanted flowers that people would see as they drove by or when they came into the shop. The first year I planted daffodils and tulips, and there were wild violets in the yard. Then I planted roses. There was a fence that had rotted posts, so instead of replacing the fence, I had it dug out, and everywhere a post had been, I planted forsythia bushes.

"That was in 1947 and the forsythia is still there, although I sold the house twelve years later."

I am one who enjoys the remnants of the forsythia hedge as I turn up Mrs. Goodwin's old street three times a week en route to regular swimming sessions at the YMCA. Until recently, I had no idea she was responsible for those bright spots, too.

Frankly, I thought she'd done quite enough when she took over the planting in a churchyard, a veterans' park, a commemorative square honoring an early civic leader, and five traffic islands strewn through two villages.

To understand why Mrs. Goodwin chose the particular spot in which to launch her campaign of brightening up dreary expanses of cement, it's necessary to know some of her history. Her story started in another small village—in Italy, outside Naples.

MARIGOLDS: 1 FRENCH, 2 AFRICAN OR AZTEC

At age seventeen, her father was an apprentice shoe-maker, working for his father. An uncle who had already left Italy tried to persuade the family to send her father, Vincenzo Ferraro, to America, the land of opportunity. He offered to sponsor his immigration and help him find work.

The hitch was that Vincenzo had a sweetheart named Lucia who was only fifteen. He didn't want to go without her, and her family vehemently opposed the wedding.

"My mother got sick brooding about my father going away," Mrs. Goodwin said, "so finally, they were allowed to get married."

The teenage newlyweds, who had never been outside their village, boarded a boat to cross the ocean. They traveled steerage, in what Mrs. Goodwin's mother would later describe as "a dark hole with animals." Everybody was sick and some people died.

The couple had been told that, when they saw "the lady in the water"—the Statue of Liberty—they would be in America. Still, they were unprepared for the confusion of Ellis Island and the teeming streets of New York.

"My uncle was waiting for them, and they got on the train and hopped from place to place around New England, staying with various relatives," Mrs. Goodwin explained. "Finally a family here in Rhode Island had a room for rent, and there were jobs for both of them in the textile mill."

Besides the mill work, Vincenzo kept up his cobbling trade, repairing shoes at night in the rented bedroom. Within a year the couple had saved enough to get their own apartment.

Eventually the Ferraros had a dozen children, of whom six survived, and Mr. Ferraro set up a shoe repair shop in the center of the village, on land leased from the railroad.

There is a traffic island in front of the place where a row of Italian-owned shops—including his—stood. That's where his daughter, Antoinetta, made her first public garden.

"I can remember what it was like so long ago. There was a store where a couple sold homemade pasta and there was a mom-and-pop variety store. At one time, there were more Italian people living in the village than any other nationality.

"Twenty years ago, I looked at the square where all this once was and it was such a mess! I thought I'd just try a little planting. I started with a few petunias around the edges, but there wasn't any water and they didn't survive. I noticed marigolds survived anywhere; they're extremely hardy. I started using them and found they're the best."

Once she started her one-woman campaign to lift

the public spirit with her summer-long floral displays, Mrs. Goodwin began to receive unsolicited suggestions of additional places she could plant. This is how it goes with public service: The public appreciates the service but doesn't actually want to pitch in and *do* any of it. And in the planting business, everybody is an instant supervisor—and an outspoken critic.

"I was at the post office one day, shortly after I'd planted the traffic island in the center of the village," Mrs. Goodwin recalled, "and this woman stopped and said, 'I think you do such a nice job downtown, wouldn't it be nice to have this place planted? It's such a disgrace.' She was asking me to do it.

"I thought, 'If you feel that way, why don't *you* do it?'"

But ugly is ugly, and Mrs. Goodwin agreed the post office traffic island *was* ugly. She also knew that nothing would be done about it unless she did it herself, so she took on another project to add to her growing list of responsibilities.

"It was all hay in there," she said. "It had grown quite high, so I put the lawnmower in the back of the car and I mowed it. It looked better. Then I talked with the State Department of Transportation about getting someone to turn over the sod for me. They refused to do anything. So I hired two boys to dig it up. Then I asked the town to bring me some loam, but they brought me gravel and just dumped it.

"I could imagine those men thinking, 'Okay, Mrs. Goodwin; you wanted it, here it is.' They didn't have any interest in what I was trying to do."

That didn't stop her; if anything, she became more convinced that her services were needed and more determined to keep planting even if she had to march toward progress dragging government officials kicking and screaming behind her. After all, she *knew* people liked what she was doing because they had told her so.

If there were a Gardeners' Hall of Fame, Antionetta Goodwin would certainly be among the first inductees, alongside Gertrude Jekyll, Euell Gibbons, Mr. Greenjeans, the Jolly Green Giant, and Peter Rabbit. Her flowery name and hardiness would probably assure Rose Kennedy a spot and, out of kindness, I think we should include Pete Rose, too, since it may be the only Hall of Fame he gets into. He'd have to start spelling his first name Peat, though.

I would nominate Mrs. Goodwin for her crusty Yankee tenacity alone. While she may have sometimes sounded strident, her intentions were pure and heartfelt. And traffic islands are not the most tranquil places to carve out gardens.

Despite intensive soil preparation at the post office crosswalk, she found her marigolds choking on car exhaust. In an effort to protect the soil and her plantings, Mrs. Goodwin tried to appropriate some abandoned curbstones to use as planters.

She didn't get them without a struggle.

When the public works director balked at giving up the granite, Mrs. Goodwin's feathers got ruffled.

"Don't play games with me!" she snapped. "They've been sitting there a hundred years. I want some of them."

The official quailed and the curbstones were delivered, some to the traffic island by the post office and others to the war memorial, where they were used to keep children from trampling the gardens.

The danger that the flowers will be stomped or, worse, driven over by careless motorists is a constant risk when you start planting in congested areas, but Mrs. Goodwin believed that the results—the pleasure derived from admirers who don't always know how the marigolds got there—made it all worthwhile.

Not even the threat of jail stopped her. That was tried, too.

"The curbings needed paint so people wouldn't drive over the plants or park in them and, of course, nobody would do anything. But I knew someone who told me where to get the shiny 'no parking' paint, and I bought some and painted the curb myself."

State highway officials, displeased with her zealousness, called to point out that what she had done was illegal and that she faced possible arrest.

"I said, 'So arrest me,'" she remembered with a smile. "I would *love* to have you arrest me."

As a gardener who is easily discouraged when plants die or people don't like what I've chosen for my own yard, I could not understand Mrs. Goodwin's resiliency, her ability to persevere at her lonely work with nothing more than an occasional kind word to sustain her. Although I'm decades younger than she was, the adversity would have been too much for me.

In fact, I have to admit that, after only three years, I stopped planting in a traffic island at the top of my own street because I was so discouraged. In the fall, a friendly neighbor and I would plant tulip, daylily, and daffodil bulbs. Then, on a spring Saturday, we'd return to cart away debris and weeds. We would add annuals such as zinnias, ageratum, and snapdragons, then spruce the whole thing up with pine bark mulch.

Practically overnight the flowers were yanked from their stems, the bulbs dug up, and the beauty replaced by beer cans. I was so angry that I refused to touch the bed again. I'm disappointed with myself for giving up, but I couldn't forgive the wanton destruction.

"You can't get discouraged," Mrs. Goodwin told me once. "If you give up, you spend the rest of your life being sorry. I believe in going on."

Planting and tending flowers in eight public spots could easily have taken its toll both financially and physically on Mrs. Goodwin, but she seemed to thrive like a fine old tree that's grown stronger and more handsome with time.

Whereas she once purchased the dozens of flats of flowers ("I figured I didn't take a vacation, so that's what I'd spend my mad money on"), later in life she started her yellow marigolds, ageratum, and blue alyssum from seed in the greenhouse on the farm that was her late husband Jack's pride and joy, a place once occupying 156 acres that she kept up, working alone. She had twenty-six acres of spruce trees although she stopped selling them as Christmas trees years ago, preferring to give them away to nursing homes and schools.

Because winter tends to hang on in our part of the world, Mrs. Goodwin used the Christmas trees as her cheer-up therapy.

For more than twenty years she hosted busloads of kindergartners who would come to her farm and make a day of selecting, then cutting down, a Christmas tree for their classroom. Dressed in snowsuits, mittens, and boots, they searched the paths until they found just the right tree. After it was cut, they would drag the tree back to the workshop, where they gathered around the old-fashioned woodstove for hot chocolate and homemade cupcakes. The tree became the centerpiece of their classroom.

If she enjoyed the smiles of adults who liked her cheery marigolds, Mrs. Goodwin loved the time she spent on the farm with the children. A single working woman until she was forty, Antoinetta had no children of her own, yet every year she got dozens.

"When you don't marry at twenty-five, after that you're not much in demand," she told me once quietly. "I missed not being married when I was very, very young, but that was during World War II and the boys were all gone. Then I was in hairdressing school and busy getting my business going, so I didn't have time to think of marriage. My sister and brothers married and had families, and their children filled that void for me."

Then, when she least expected it, along came Jack Goodwin, a strapping Irish widower who arrived at her beauty shop asking that she dye his handlebar mustache black for a role he had in a community theater production. There was an instant attraction and, before long, a surprised Antoinetta Ferraro found herself married.

For three years they weekended at Jack's farm, returning to her house in town so she could keep the beauty shop going. When it got to be too much, they moved permanently to the farm, where they lived for ten years before her husband died of cancer.

"We couldn't have been happier here," she remem-

Antoinetta Goodwin

bered, sitting at a kitchen window that looked out on a pond full of ducks and acres of evergreens.

The front of the farmhouse was made of granite from the quarry below; the bedroom windows upstairs were once part of the old barn. A year after their marriage, they began planting Christmas trees, starting in a far-off field. Within two years they'd put in 6,000 seedlings; after five years they began selling trees.

"We had the best business," said Mrs. Goodwin, who lived alone on the farm for twenty-nine years.

"I can't think, 'Now I'm seventy-six. Why plant any more trees?' And I told my nieces not to ask me how old I am anymore because pretty soon they'd be saying, 'Don't you think you should stop planting marigolds in the traffic islands?'

"I don't believe that's how life is. If you enjoy something, just *do* it!"

Before I met Mrs. Goodwin, I'd never seen gardens in crosswalks or plastic chickens wearing sweaters and waving flags. Now I can't imagine life in our community without them.

Antoinetta Goodwin died last May at the age of 83. Her family, the beloved nieces, brought her costumed chickens to the funeral home and set them up near the head of the coffin. To ensure that Mrs. Goodwin's devotion to her community would never be forgotten the Town of South Kingstown planted shrubs, daylilies, and perennials in the long traffic island by the post office—the spot where I first saw Mrs. Goodwin at work—and dedicated an engraved bronze plaque set in granite in her memory. After all her little go-rounds with governmental hierarchy she would undoubtedly be rather surprised by this tribute and certainly very pleased.

NO, THE *OTHER* MARTHA

From time to time, usually when I'm loading my carriage with frozen yogurt in the supermarket or awaiting treatment in the hospital emergency room, some fathead will say: "Oh! Are you THE Martha?"

And I will smile faintly and admit that I am.

And then this person will say, glancing at my cart or my cardiogram, "Martha STEWART! I read you all the time!"

Thanks a lot.

It's easy, of course, to see how a person would mistake us, what with her being tall, thin, blonde, wildly talented, and fabulously wealthy, and me being short, dumpy, dark-haired (with a little assist from my stylist the phenomenal Fred), moderately skilled, and pathetically poor.

When I still lived down South, where I also wrote a column that appeared bearing a photograph that looked more or less like me, there were times I'd get called Martha White, the name of the flour manufacturer best known as a Grand Ole Opry sponsor.

It's a curse being named Martha.

I'm sure Martha Stewart feels the same way. There are probably countless times when she gets mistaken for me and, maintaining her blinding smile, she sets to deadheading the roses with renewed vigor.

The thing that really irks me about the other Martha—besides the fact that she has her own magazine and has created an entire empire and owns a mansion in Connecticut and works in the garden without ever raising a bead of perspiration—is her seemingly boundless creativity.

How *does* she manage to think up all those things to do with dried-up plants that to anyone else, me included, appear to have compost heap written all over them? Instead of being tossed out as flowers that have outlived their beauty, they become wreaths and swags and are woven into baskets or painted and glued onto centerpieces.

For all I know she's busy at this very moment making hats out of croaked chrysanthemums.

Me, I believe that for everything there is a season and, when the posies are pooped, the season's over. So long, sayonara, see you next year. Time for everyone to take a well-deserved rest. Everyone, that is, except the other Martha. She appears never to rest, always having some other mountain to climb, some further frontier to explore. (Now that they've found evidence of life on Mars she'll probably be devising ways to perk the place up and adorn it with cute little cut-outs reading "Welcome to Our Planet.")

My feeling is that, even if I had a scintilla of Martha

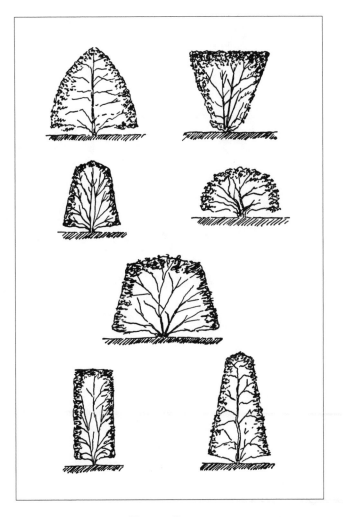

HEDGE FORMS

Stewart's creativity, I'd be doomed to obscurity because I wouldn't have the energy to carry out a major project. Martha has what I lack: a staff.

It must be a snap to come up with clever ideas for labor-intensive desserts and pressed-flower engagement books and Christmas trees made of handblown glass that you've cranked out yourself in your very own workshop when you have a regiment of laborers tending to all the details.

Knowing that all the heavy stuff is being done by underlings endows a person with a certain freedom, a *joie de vivre* as it were, to let the old juices flow. Oh that I had such freedom. My juices are usually what I'm stewing in.

For instance, while Martha Stewart throws a pot in which she'll be planting a priceless seedling from her showcase garden to give as a housewarming gift, I will be throwing a pot in anger because the seedling has expired.

Whereas Martha Stewart might be pruning her shrubs into delightful topiary versions of animals, I'd be more likely to turn my evergreens into a tribute to boot camp, clipped back to screaming closeness.

As Martha Stewart whipped up a twelve-course dinner for a hundred of her closest chums, I'd be setting out a six-pack and a half-dozen chicken fingers for me and the dog.

Other than our names—and Smith and Stewart are not that dissimilar, either—the other Martha and I have precious little in common. We both love gardens, of course, but mine does not resemble Sissinghurst; we both love food, but Martha prefers to cook while I, well, I would rather eat.

We both appreciate the printed word but I don't own a magazine and, if I did, it would be more aptly called *Martha Smith Existing* or *Martha Smith: You Call THIS Living?*

Nonetheless, it's nice to think that some people imagine us to be one and the same person, that they are unable to discern between the painfully chic and the merely painful. However, just in case you're not sure which Martha is which, you might want to take the following short quiz so that next time you see one of us in the supermarket you'll know with certainty who it is.

Martha Stewart finds potpourri delightful for:
    a) adding texture to a room
    b) suffusing the air with a light fragrance
    c) displaying in an heirloom bowl
    d) giving to friends, after making the mixture from her own flowers

Martha Smith finds potpourri delightful for:

a) grinding into the rug on the spot where the dog threw up

Martha Stewart's mentors were:
a) Julia Child and Sister Parish
b) Craig Claiborne and Edith Wharton

Martha Smith's mentors were:
a) Colonel Sanders and Chuck E. Cheese
b) Sara Lee and the Salvation Army

Martha Stewart's idea of the perfect meal is:
home-baked bread made with wheat grown on her estate; venison stew created from a deer she bagged herself, with one perfect, painless shot between the eyes; deep dish apple pie made with apples from her own orchard, all served on ceramic pots made in her own kiln before a crackling fire of wood she chopped before breakfast

Martha Smith's idea of the perfect meal is:
anything somebody else cooks

If called upon to provide a last-minute gift for a girlfriend, Martha Stewart will:
a) shear a sheep, spin the wool, and knit a sweater
b) send three dozen perfect, long-stemmed roses personally selected from her own garden

c) create a decorative pillow by stitching the recipient's name on antique velvet fabric stuffed with feathers collected from her own flock of geese

If called upon to provide a last-minute gift for a girlfriend, Martha Smith will:

a) order up a singing male strip-o-gram and a naughty card

When Martha Stewart is in the garden she is always:

a) decked out in Donna Karan and using designer tools from chic garden boutiques
b) totally calm and unruffled
c) as knowledgeable as Vita Sackville-West and Gertrude Jekyll combined

When Martha Smith is in the garden she is always:

a) wearing torn tee-shirts and slacks and muddy shoes and using tools salvaged from yard sales
b) a totally icky sweatball
c) as knowledgeable as Jerry West and Heckle & Jeckle

Martha Stewart's idea of the perfect garden party is:

a) tea and cucumber sandwiches among the roses
b) mint juleps in the gazebo, covered by bougainvillea

   c) a picnic lunch under tents, surrounded by hibiscus and mock orange

Martha Smith's idea of the perfect garden party is:

   a) a bottle of wine, a blanket, and Mel Gibson under a weeping willow
   b) having all her friends over to weed
   c) Chinese take-out for two, shared with the dog

Martha Stewart's very favorite flower is:

   herself

Martha Smith's very favorite flower is:

   the rose, after the bloom is off, which is kind of like herself

So there you have it, the definitive guide to why the two Marthas are so very, very different. And were you to ask her what flower she'd like to be, as Barbara Walters inquired of Katharine Hepburn in a discussion of trees, her answer would surely be: the money plant.

But, then, in a way she already is.

SPRING HOPES ETERNAL: CONFESSIONS OF A CATALOGUE QUEEN

No *Playgirl* centerfold moves me like a glossy picture of grandiflora rose bushes blazing with seductive color. No country mansion featured in *House Beautiful* inspires my desire as much as photos of a mixed lupine collection or violet clematis surging over a stone wall. No *Vogue* layout of Paris fashions stirs my longings as much as when I look at perfect perennial borders that *can be mine* if I order early (while supplies last!).

So, of course, I order. Everything. It's a weakness I'd feel a lot worse about if I hadn't discovered that veteran gardeners who have been nurturing their beds for forty years are *also* suckers for catalogues. Show me an amateur grower and I'll show you someone who absolutely cannot live without ordering something new every season, regardless of how many flowers are already in place and how much additional work will be required.

It is the secret curse of garden addicts and all of us should probably join Catalogues Anonymous to lend support to each other—except, of course, the minute we got together we'd be filling out order forms.

As far as I've been able to tell, there is no more persuasive promise than that of the garden flower-and-ornament catalogue. Forget chances to win a million bucks from a magazine subscription company. Never mind a megabucks jackpot that could make you richer than Donald Trump. Ignore those guarantees of instant weight loss, instant wrinkle removal, and instant marriage proposals.

Without question the most cunning salesmen on the face of the earth are the purveyors of these seductive catalogues. Why? They have a keen grasp of human nature and they know that timing is everything.

In early January, just as you're staring dolefully out the window at a slate-gray sky, a salt-encrusted street, and a pile of dirty snow and taking yet another antidepressant—which, in my case, is a Sara Lee triple-decker coconut cake eaten in its entirety fresh from the box—the mailman arrives to save you from yourself.

He'll deliver you into the hands of perdition in the form of a faraway nursery that you can call direct via a toll-free number and, clutching credit card in hand, say, "Yes. I'll take three of everything, please."

The way to hell is paved with beautifully glossy flower catalogues that arrive in full, glorious, better-than-living color just when you can't face another bleak winter moment. And I should know, since I am prepared to lay claim to the title Queen of the Bulb Catalogue Clients. Without my devoted patronage I daresay the entire Netherlands would go bankrupt because, each

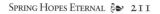

"THE WAY TO HELL IS PAVED WITH BEAUTIFULLY,
GLOSSY FLOWER CATALOGUES THAT ARRIVE IN FULL,
GLORIOUS, BETTER-THAN-LIVING COLOR. . ."

fall, I faithfully order another zillion Holland tulip bulbs to add to the zillion I've already got.

The same can be said of my steadfast loyalty to Burpee, Park Seed, White Flower Farm, Wayside Gardens, and all the specialty houses of the American Northwest whose propagation of fantastic new dahlia species creates colors I *must have*! I've even weakened in the face of the pricey accessories of Smith & Hawken and Gardener's Eden.

For someone to whom the door of gardening possibilities has been thrown open there is never a moment's hesitation in ordering anything that catches my fancy. Never mind that a plant requires semitropical temperatures and I live in frigid New England, where our growing season lasts about three hours. Never mind that the plant will need to be taken up and separated every year; that's what the implements in the toolshed are for, right?

Never mind that I've already got more beds to tend than Holiday Inn. Who needs a social life? Never mind that I've got a cash flow situation that makes the federal trade deficit look like small-stakes bingo. Besides my local banker, who cares anyhow?

All of these factors are beside the point because: *I cannot resist!*

In me—and countless other winter-weary gardeners—these dream-sellers find the perfect suckers. They catch us when we are most vulnerable and zap us with a shot of photographic floral adrenalin. We gaze longingly at the opulent color photographs, read descriptions of the endless splendor and productivity of the plants, and find they tug at our heartstrings—and our purse strings.

The garden catalogue is the ultimate fantasy source. I caress its pages and drool, dreaming of formal English gardens overflowing with everything pictured. The prose sings to me and I croon back.

I, too, will exercise *a break-through in miniature day-lilies!* I will see them born in such profusion that strangers will swoon and crowds will gather to applaud. My garden will be home to the latest exciting new imported European bulb, *superior in flower production!* The sumptuous color will dazzle, the exotic fragrance will lie upon the air like a scented mist. The neighbors will waltz about the streets like Disney characters in *Fantasia*.

My *aristocratic bulbs* will multiply with each passing year, making a *magnificent colony* of snooty beauty, a floral Beverly Hills. My garden will have nothing that is not *extremely rare, unusually attractive, vividly beautiful*. (Sometimes, when I am transported while reading these catalogue descriptions, I wonder if they were written by Robin Leach, the bellowing TV visitor of the "Rich and Famous.")

My peonies, reflecting my own persona, will be *large yet delicate*! My daffodils will be lush, splendid, giant, and multiple-award winners—truly for the *discerning gardener*! My jonquils will be intriguing, my hydrangeas fuller, more decorative, and capable of producing *a spectacular show!*

My hyacinths will bloom in *heart-lifting jubilant colors* in midspring!

Dizzy with the enticements held out by this beguiling prose, I turn to the last page and follow that most urgent of advisories: *The best time to order is now!*

Of course it is. It is the deadliest part of winter, the time when, as the mailman staggers off with their catalogues, the purveyors of garden dreams sit back smugly and say, "Gotcha!"

Invariably these harbingers of bankruptcy—filled with bulbs, seeds, shrubs, and garden embellishments—start showing up smack in the middle of the post-Christmas doldrums, a time when I'm considering lying down in the middle of the road in hopes that a ten-ton snowplow will drive over me.

Every page is filled with dazzling blossoms that beckon to me, whispering, "Buy me! Buy me!" In my weakened condition, I do. With a slightly crazed laugh, I fill out the order-now-pay-later form, sending for multiples of nearly everything. If I'm having a really bad day and require instant gratification, I use the toll-free phone number—even though it will be four full months before I can plant anything because the ground in these parts resembles the tundra until mid-May.

Only after I've made my selections do I realize I'll need to take a night job pumping gas to pay off the credit card bill. It's also possible that I've ordered enough flowers to fill the botanical gardens and make them seem, well, overdone.

Do I care about any of this? No. Do I care about cost? It is to laugh.

I want the *exciting and unique plants* that these catalogues have promised me. I want all that is *vigorous, vivid*, and covered by *Visa*! I want to *remember what I've ordered*, but by spring, I can't.

Because I always feel so stupid at 1) being plunged into the depths of bulb blackout by the unexpected arrival of the order, and 2) not recalling precisely where I thought the flowers might look nice when I phoned the nursery in a fever of enthusiasm, I search for empathy from other similarly afflicted growers.

I found one man who confessed to having so many flowerbeds and vegetable patches around his faux farmhouse that he was forced to plow and weed by moonlight. Other addicts admit to a system of caroming between their own backyard gardens and plots they've planted on borrowed property. They *had* to expand, they say, because they just couldn't stop acquiring new things. As one plant packrat explained, "Even if you've

HYDRANGEAS

already got sixty-three varieties of something and, suddenly, a sixty-fourth variety is on the market, then there's no question—you've got to have it."

That accounts for why, in most catalogues from speciality houses such as iris or dahlia propagators, there's always a page of new arrivals, some costing as much as fifty bucks for a single bulb. For the nursery, it's the best of situations since the supply is limited and the demand, among discriminating aficionados (read the Truly Possessed), is steady.

At least I'm not guilty of this sort of reckless spending. Since I'd rather have the quantity (until it arrives by the truckload), I refuse to spend more on a flower than the cost of a nice restaurant dessert. I'm aided in this resolve by the fact that there's no particular plant to which I'm overly devoted. I like them all.

When the cartons of bulbs and tubers and seedlings begin arriving—invariably too early, no matter how often I admonish the nursery that if they ship before May 1 I'll have to jackhammer through the soil—it's like Christmas, with the slight hitch that I'm Santa and I can't remember what I've given myself.

Besides a lot of instant work, that is.

Not only do the bulb boxes arrive unexpectedly, they arrive all at once in the sort of deluge that causes the deliveryman to stagger up the front steps cursing me soundly. They also show up with large printed instructions that say, "*Plant immediately!*"

With boxes stacked up so high that the dog has to pole-vault her way out the door, planting is the quickest way to rid the house of chaos. Unfortunately, there's almost no time after work to get home, change clothes, and make even a dent in the project.

Quick thinking is needed, and what better strategy than the old Instant Illness ploy? Placing a hanky over the receiver and pinching my nose slightly for extra effect, I phone the boss's secretary.

"Yez, it'z me," I croak. "I've got one of these forty-eight hour things thass going aroun . . ." I look at the mountain of crated seedlings and bulbs.

"It may be one of those seventy-two hour things."

"Oh, you poor dear!" murmurs the compassionate voice on the other end, making me feel—briefly—guilty. "Drink lots of juice and stay in bed."

And so I do: I stay in the rose bed and the dahlia bed, the shade bed and the perennial bed. I am there until the order is planted, usually necessitating a long weekend, which is normally the time it takes most employees faking an illness to recover.

Besides the usual business of tilling the soil, making rows, and digging holes, there are other considerations. There is the sudden realization that I have no peat moss or bagged topsoil—an annual "surprise" along the same lines as the arrival of my income tax form—and that I'll have to make a furtive trip to the supply house, praying that nobody I know spots me.

There's also the business of mulch switching—replacing winter hay with summer bark—which is, I'm sorry to say, mulch ado.

But eventually, when all the work is done, I allow myself the luxury of sitting back and thumbing through the catalogues offering all the things I cannot afford.

I can say with absolute honesty that it's not possible, when faced with so much temptation, to overestimate the "cheapness factor." It's my basic frugality—and a tendency to faint at the sight of price tags bearing more digits than my Social Security number—that keeps me from sending off for $500 teak benches, $300 imported English stone urns, or fountains costing roughly the same amount as a new luxury car.

That doesn't mean my imagination can't run wild.

If I really wanted to live it up, I'd grab the phone and call Clapper's, the luxury garden decor supplier in Newton, Massachusetts. I'd say, "Send me the 72-inch Lutyens Garden Bench, please. Yes, the one for $1,495 that's a copy of *the original*! by Sir Edwin Lutyens. Perhaps you'd better make that two. And throw in a couple of those Wimbleton coffee tables at $220."

If I stayed on the wire long enough, I could wind up with a lot of other items with British names: a $550

Arundel Table, a $350 Edinburg Table, a $496 Balmoral Table, a $275 London Armchair. Then I could switch to Continental Europe and get myself a $995 Roman Garden Parasol, made by *Italian Craftsmen in Milan*! To make the picture complete, I'd have to have the $495 Commodore Steamer Chair, on which I'd recline in certain discomfort as a result of my nagging conscience and the bare wooden slats pinching my flesh.

From Smith & Hawken or Gardener's Eden I could choose a variety of tools I never knew I needed, such as a $47.25 grafting knife and sheath, a $48.50 imported English bulb planter, a $69.95 border fork, a $113.85 long-handled pruner, a $295 faux terra cotta planter prompting the supplier to sing a chorus of "Faux She's a Jolly Good Fellow." Or I might wish to consider any number of pretentiously advertised implements from the London firm of Jenks & Cattell, presumably suppliers to dukes, duchesses, counts, no-accounts, and the entire cast of *Upstairs, Downstairs.*

Frankly, none of this suits my taste, never mind my budget. Moreover, I'll never understand how anyone gets his money's worth from a garden bench; everyone knows that gardeners have no time to sit around lollygagging.

The minute I stop for a breather, eighteen Japanese beetles show up with dinner reservations for my rose

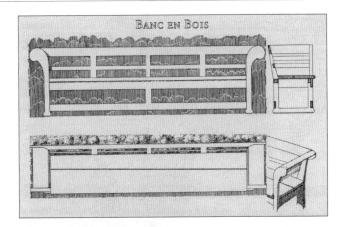

Benches

bushes while three new species of vining weeds try to strangle the snapdragons. The main purpose benches serve is as a restroom for birds who, generally speaking, don't really care what sort of expensive wood they're soiling. Fowl are, I've always found, foul about such things.

As far as I'm concerned, let the birds mess up something cheap, like the new trifles I've permitted myself in the faux marble, which are, in other words, cement. I have effigies of bunnies, a Scottie, and an Airedale puppy, a lounging cat who resembles my own lazy pet, a young girl with a basket of flowers, and a maiden with two clinging cherubs who appear to be angling for a look up her dress.

I've got a big garden on both sides of the house, so these things (none of which cost more than fifty-five bucks) are placed with the goal of surprising and delighting the casual stroller. When tired of walking, visitors can plop down in my sky-blue metal reproduction art deco chairs, bought on sale for $19.95 (some assembly required).

I am the sort of gardener who likes simple woodland creatures, sitting individually. Others, however, prefer theme-park-like sets of marching elves, families of ceramic skunks and chickens, wooden ducks whose wings flail when the wind blows, and geese who inflate like an airport wind sock in a stiff breeze.

My favorite garden of outlandish adornments is in Bob Rossi's backyard in Cranston, Rhode Island, where he has been hiding the chassis of antique Metropolitan cars for years. Rossi and his large teenage sons are almost always working on one of their five egg-shaped Metropolitans—a car built in England by Nash from 1954 to 1962. Because he always needs extras for parts—but doesn't want to create a neighborhood eyesore—Rossi buries the surplus Metropolitans and plants arborvitae, flowering shrubs, and vining roses around them.

In Rossi's garden, many a casual visitor has walked around the swimming pool and sniffed the fragrant blooms before noticing they're growing through the windshield and empty engine cavity of a funny little car. It is, I think, Rossi's own definition of an English car park.

Among other garden decorations, old-timers are loyal to the enormous glitter balls on pedestals, and plastic daisies and miniature windmills that spin like roulette wheels. Wooden cutouts have become popular in recent years, especially life-size cows, fuzzy sheep, and enormous fannies of women bending over. And let us not forget the artistic hose attachments, which include effigies of Ronald Reagan, Elvis, Liberace, Moses, and Pope John Paul II, whose upraised, spouting hands appear to be sprinkling holy water over the plants.

Religious shrines are always among the preferred

garden doodads of the devout, with Our Lady of the Bathtub (also known in some areas as the Virgin on the Half-Shell) leading the way. St. Francis is big, along with sculptures of children kneeling in prayer. It occurs to me, however, that a lot of other saints are being ignored.

I'd like to remedy that with a

Guide to Garden Saints:

St. Elmo's Fire. Patron saint of hot peppers.

St. Bernard. Protector of dogwood.

St. Louis Armstrong. Patron saint of trumpet lilies.

Susan St. James. Overseer of wildflowers and organic gardens.

Bells of St. Mary's. The perfect shrine for your coral bells.

When the Saints Go Marching In. In homage to lady's slippers.

St. Petersburg. Patron saint of sunflowers.

St. Cloud. Sacred guardian of rain lilies.

Eva Marie Saint. Protectress of the Blazing Star-flower.

Saint Elsewhere. Guardian of transplanted flowers.

Sault St. Marie. The perfect spot to freesia.

Saints Preserve Us. A shrine for vegetables to be canned.

Having a few bits of statuary sitting around has proved useful since I've never quite mastered the business of spacing. I unfailingly place things too far apart, fearing that if I don't, they'll become crowded and crush each other. I always like to plant things like the old-time Soviets do—on a five-year plan, imagining that, at the end of that time, everything will look like it does in the catalogues.

In retrospect—and considering the extreme circumstances of my panic when the bulb orders arrive—I think I behave as decently as possible: I never push my luck and am back at the grindstone by Monday, looking haggard enough to make the phony flu seem plausible.

"How do you feel?" chirps a co-worker.

"Uggghhh," I moan, with genuine feeling.

"What happened to your fingernails?" she asks, glancing at the formerly manicured, polished ovals that are now quarter-inch long stubs that appear to have been through a Cuisinart at chop-and-dice speed.

"Nerves," I say quickly. "I get very nervous being confined to bed. It's soooo boring, and I can't wait to get up and get back here to work."

"It's probably stress," she says, nodding sympathetically. "Maybe you should take some time off, just for yourself."

Of course, there is no time to spend on yourself once spring arrives, with its eternal hope of renewal and its endless tasks. Confronted with dozens of new plants taking their place among the existing, already formidable flowers, it is always unclear whether there will be time to actually tend them.

I am always surprised at how much more of the three Ws (weeding, watering, whining) I've assigned myself by greedily ordering.

I'm also flabbergasted that, somehow, I *do* manage to get everything into the ground in some semblance of order. Okay, so I sometimes lose the popsickle-stick markers identifying the plants; I can always figure out what they are when they bloom. And I *have* been known on occasion to confuse the ends of a bare root plant and push it into the dirt head first. This happened with an order of dianthus that arrived looking like so many dried-up paint brushes. I'm not sure any of it would have lived even if I had managed to get it planted right side up.

As spring progresses and the planting fever subsides, I fall into a daily routine: After work each day, I change into ragged gardening clothes and inspect the beds to see what's poking through the ground and, later, what's starting to bud. In the beginning I'm always vigilant about weeds and spend part of each evening pouncing on dandelions and chokeweeds, digging them up with a trowel and wondering if it might not be simpler to set off a small explosive charge.

I'm aided on these deceptively simple early spring evenings by my new fox terrier, Delia, who trots beside me, stomping on whatever happens to be emerging from its winter sleep. As the season heats up and flowers begin popping up right and left—along with hordes of weeds and insects—I'm on my knees doing serious work with a wonderful two-headed hand tool that has a small spade on one side and a three-pronged cultivator fork on the other.

Since I have a basic aversion to sweat, finding that it inevitably leads to personal discomfort as well as a larger amount of laundry, I try to spend the intensely humid month of August tending the garden in the cooler early-morning hours before work and in the twilight of weekends.

When I'm working the twilight shift, Delia also changes her realm of responsibility, switching to a supervisory position overseeing my efforts.

Her very favorite thing, however, is the evening watering ritual. This is when Terrier Frenzy sets in and she becomes a combination kangaroo-snapping turtle, leaping into the air and clacking her jaws under the sprinkler in an attempt to catch the water. I have to seize her and drag her indoors because if I let her stay out there she would jump and growl and snap—and look totally ridiculous—until she was nothing but a sodden mass. One of us is enough and I'm already soaked from working.

I feel in general, though, that I'm getting off light with this small show of pet agitation. It's not the same, certainly, as having a bevy of youngsters yelling, "Mom, we're hungry!" just as I settled into some quietly soothing communion with the cleome. Being single and childless, I have the extra time to spend nurturing the garden and being nurtured by it.

Whether I would have *quite* so much nourishment were it not for the cleverness of garden catalogue producers, is in doubt. I'm inclined to think I'd still somehow manage to buy more flowers than I really need—it would just take me longer to acquire them if I had to drive everywhere and pick them up.

I guess you could say the catalogues are helping me save gas money.

DON'T BUG ME!

Once the catalogue invasion has been quelled and the new candidates are competing for glory and honor among previous years' blossoms, there is a second assault to be anticipated: the arrival of the loathsome insect brigades.

Speaking from personal experience, I can say there is nothing more alarming than the discovery that *something is eating your flowers!* Worse than knowing it's the hideous, hard-shelled Japanese beetles, with their insatiable appetite for rose petals and anything else they can pillage, is the uncertainty of not knowing what is attacking the fragile blooms you've been waiting for all year.

This is where Maggie Hogan and other experts affiliated with the Cooperative Extension Services of state land-grant colleges come in: At no charge to the taxpayers, these horticultural sleuths will track down and identify the culprit that's causing blight and destruction to plant life. It matters not the size of the crop: The extension service helps everyone from major commercial growers to backyard dabblers like me. Staff members will analyze your soil and check your garden plan to make sure you have assigned your plants to the correct location and given them enough space.

They're also on hand to examine leaves afflicted by mysterious fungi and to recommend ways to minimize crop loss caused by disease and pests.

It was in connection with my gladioli that I first called Maggie at the University of Rhode Island's extension center to say, "HELP!"

Something was chewing on my flowers and rummaging through the broad-leafed plants like a vegetarian pigging out at a salad bar. The delicate green fronds were becoming so riddled they looked as if they had been caught in some military cross fire.

Since there wasn't much Maggie and company could do without a specimen to scrutinize, I set up an observation post at the back door, lying in wait for the scoundrels.

Quite by accident, it turned out, I caught one of them in the act as I was taking the dog out for her pre-bedtime pit stop. As I stood by the gate, an ethereal gray presence came flapping from the foliage, practically under my nose, sending me to a record height in the standing high jump.

"AHA!" I cried, once I'd caught my breath. "Now I've got you!"

In a trice I had grabbed the fluttering thing and held it in my palm, while I searched with the other hand for a lidded jar. By the time I found one, I also discovered that this particular insect leaves a dusty residue on whatever it touches—in this case my hand.

"Yuck!" I said, grimacing. "This is disgusting!"

I did not know the meaning of disgusting until I watched Maggie, part of a much larger team of resource people, hard at work. They are surrounded by yucky things every day, and seem to like the yuck.

"Staring down a microscope at a disgusting creature isn't much fun," admits Maggie who, with her short, curly blond hair and tendency to buzz around the lab, resembles a fuzzy bumblebee. "But there's a lot of satisfaction in identifying what it is. I feel like a detective because, when you get something in that isn't immediately identifiable, you start with all the possibilities and then begin eliminating until you've got it pinpointed. What it amounts to is that I'm testing my knowledge against the existence of this pest. And the people who bring these things in are almost like children in their amazement when I'm able to tell them what it is and what to do about it. They act like I'm God or something."

Of course, this is entirely understandable. The amateur grower is inclined to embrace anyone who knows how to prevent a scourge from swarming through the garden and murdering all the baby plants. I felt a twinge of religious ardor when Maggie was able to tell me that

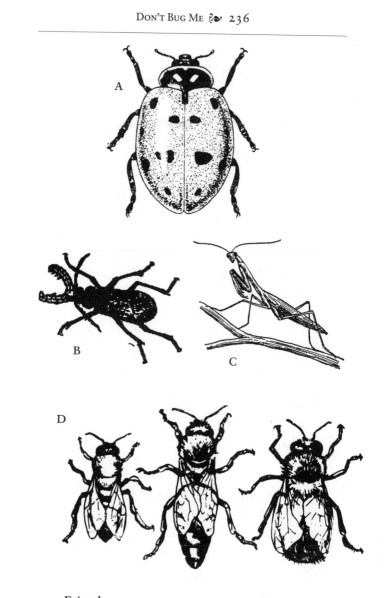

Friend: A. LADY BUG, B.BENEFICIAL BEETLE ,
C. PRAYING MANTIS, D. BEES (WORKER, QUEEN, DRONE)

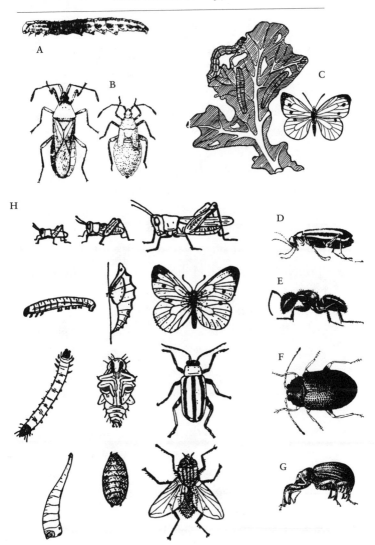

Foe: A. STALK BORER, B. SQUASH BUG, C. CABBAGE
WORM & BUTTERFLY, D. BLISTER BEETLE, E. ANT,
F. POTATO FLEA BEETLE, G. PEPPER WEEVIL,
H. METAMORPHOSIS (GRASSHOPPER, BUTTERFLY, BEETLE, FLY)

the silver fuzzy-wuzzy was, in fact, a cabbage moth—a bug with a fondness for leafy flowers and vegetables. "Cabbage worms (or moths) eat huge holes in everything, leaving nothing but the skeleton of a plant behind," she added. She suggested a few ways of getting rid of them. One was to get hold of some Trichogramma parasitic wasps, who lay their eggs on top of the cabbage moth eggs and prevent them from hatching.

"Just what I need," I sighed. "More bugs."

I opted for choice number two: Dusting with Rotenone, a very mild vegetable-based insecticide derived from the root of the derris plant. I got hold of some, sprinkled it around and discovered that the worms no longer found my flowers so tasty.

"Our stand on pesticides," Maggie explained, "is to use as little as possible but spray when necessary. We also push as many organic controls as possible." Some are amazingly old-fashioned yet effective.

Among the organic sprays are Pyrethrum, made from painted daisy blossoms, and a soupy mixture made from steeping chrysanthemum leaves in water. In his book *Kitchen Herbs*, Connecticut herb gardener Sal Gilbertie gives a recipe for repelling insects, called Nana's Bug Juice, that involves blending garlic, cayenne pepper, and cider vinegar, straining the concoction through cheesecloth, then applying it to plants with a mist sprayer.

Whipping up a batch of mild liquid soap and spraying it on plants is said to smother earwigs, thrips, and aphids.

Planting certain flowers and vegetables to ward off insects is also effective. Many people plant marigolds around their vegetables because they produce a thick, pungent smell similar to citronella that repels many insects.

Conversely, flower gardeners have found that planting garlic and onions around beds of particularly tender flowers keeps away bugs—as well as vampires.

If you want to fight fire with fire, there are lots of helpful insects which keep down the population of the naughty bugs you *don't* want in the garden. Ladybugs and green lacewings love to munch on aphids, and praying mantises are fond of feasting on nasty beasties.

Throughout the years, I think there have been almost as many favorite remedies for killing beetles as there have been gardeners anxious to try them out. A friend said that one of his earliest childhood recollections is of his grandfather going about his Saturday morning ritual of heating warm, soapy water and heading out to the grape arbor, where he methodically examined every leaf, flicking beetles to their sudsy grave at each step.

"He would set his teeth in a grimace and go out there without fail. It was as though, if he couldn't control other lousy things that went on in life, by God he could at least protect his grapes!"

It was with the same feeling of outraged sensibility that I remember finding long-awaited roses shredded before the buds had opened. And, when I pried the splintered petals apart, I was revolted to find a dozen greedy iridescent beetles, like so many Darth Vaders, climbing all over each other in their effort to grab a snack while there was something left. I called over the fence to the neighborhood gardening guru and got his advice: A coffee can with plain cooking oil or kerosene would do the trick.

Although it was too late to save my beloved roses, I got a definite feeling of satisfaction as I dumped the gorgers into the mess. I'm sure they didn't appreciate that it was low in saturated fats since they have no hearts anyway.

For those who like to keep up on the latest in the insect world—and believe me, the longer you grow, the more obsessed you become with blotting out the lives of wicked bugs—there is a catalogue devoted entirely to safe garden products. It's called *Gardens Alive!* and it's produced by the Natural Gardening Research Center in Indiana, a sort of supply house for Rambos who've declared war on gnawing creatures.

There are, for instance, two pages devoted to insect traps for garden and orchard. A star of the collection is the devious red sphere trap, which looks like a ripe apple and gives the come-on to apple maggot flies—which become hopelessly caged and die. HA-HA! If you want to increase your chances of success, you might also want to invest in sticky tangle-tape and apple maggot lures, which are apparently, to maggots as a sultry perfume is to hapless suitors.

My favorite among the murderous appliances is the Pheromone Lure Trap, which magically imitates the aromatic sex lure of most insects. It summons them to what they think is an orgy—only to make sure they never party in your garden again!

I sent off for one of these and, murmuring "Come up and see me sometime, big boys," cheerfully installed it in the rose and dahlia beds. Sure enough, because I started *before* the bugs had invaded and laid eggs, I was able to minimize damage by the promised high percentage—including imprisonment of that most horrible of plant diners, the Japanese beetle.

According to Maggie Hogan, Japanese beetles rate somewhere just below the plague as far as gardeners are concerned. They're in the super-enemy category, she says, along with aphids, moths, maggots, weevils, mites, borers, slugs, and worms. Many insect samples arrive at her office in various panic-inspired ways. Because I live near the university, I was able to present myself on her doorstep with my cabbage moth carefully packaged in a small cardboard box. Other growers are not so thoughtful.

"If people call in advance we tell them to put their samples in a pill bottle," she says, noting that things often show up looking like they've been put through a blender before mailing.

"Just this morning I got this piece of Kleenex in an envelope. There was some kind of splotch on it that must have been a bug at one time but, after going through the postal meter, there was nothing left."

Worse still, she says, was the farmer who boxed up an entire rotting head of cabbage—filled with insects—and sent it in. As with other arriving mail, it got stacked in a pile awaiting its turn.

"We noticed this terrible smell that got progressively worse. The box sat there, meanwhile, stinking up the place until finally we opened it. You want to talk about absolutely revolting?"

Maggie says her office receives approximately 600 specimens a year, including bugs people want to get rid of, and plants that need to be identified, fifty percent of which arrive between June and August.

With a background in plant science and ornamental horticulture, she feels that her work pulls all her training together and enables her to offer real relief to gardeners in distress.

"When people want a quick fix, they call us for help,"

she says, adding that, besides emergency aid in terms of recommending insect repellents, the extension service offers guidance for long-term prevention and maintenance.

Another event that sends growers into a tailspin is any sort of announcement that a new variety of insect has appeared *anywhere in the Northern Hemisphere!* Even if the bug has been sighted no nearer than 3,000 miles away, everyone is sure they've got it in their garden. These are the times, says Maggie, that try the patience mightily, because the phone rings off the hook with gardeners who are genuinely—albeit needlessly—concerned.

It's not unlike the worried mother who, reading about some new strain of influenza, starts imagining that her own child has a fever and suspicious symptoms.

Personally I find that it's all I can do to wrangle with the gardening problems I *do* have without courting trouble that, for now at least, hasn't afflicted me. After all, the phrase "common or garden variety" could just as well have been inspired by the ordinary old insects that show up to nibble—the Oriental invaders, the moths and green flies. When you have these to contend with, you don't need exotic species.

I should note here that, besides the Japanese beetles and cabbage worms who like to chow down on the lushest foliage in my garden, I have another particularly annoying pest that prefers morsels of a plumper, juicier variety. In short, me.

I refer, of course, to mosquitoes, those B-52 bombers that turn every twilight garden into a flesh munch-a-thon. It never fails that I find some small chore that absolutely must be done in that brief time between work and bedtime. Just as I set out with shears to nip off the deadheads of dahlias and roses or to tie up a drooping plant, I find myself attacked by sneaky mosquitoes whose only warning is the loud droning hum they make just before plunging their barbs into me.

There are some fairly simple precautions that, when used together, make for effective bite prevention: Wearing long-sleeved shirts and long pants will keep exposed areas to a minimum—although if it's hot and you're sweating, more mosquitoes will make a beeline, pardon the expression, to your locale. Generously spritzing any skin that's showing with an over-the-counter insect repellent will discourage most mosquitoes, as well as any amorous humans.

Avon also sells something called Skin-So-Soft bath oil that's getting wide acclaim for its hidden benefit: It's a terrific insect repellent. While company officials initially seemed embarrassed by this revelation, they concluded that a sale was a sale so they might as well be good sports about it.

I, meanwhile, stumbled upon something else that's

provided an effective means of keeping mosquitoes—
and the neighbors—at a distance. It involves Delia and
me dressing up in matching dragonfly costumes during
the height of the insect season.

The whole idea (and fashion breakthrough) was
inspired by the *Gardener's Supply* catalogue which—
besides the standard accoutrements of sprinkler systems, space-age compost makers, and a variety of tools
that, should your garden fail, might prove useful in a
career of breaking and entering—featured the following insect-control item: an electronic device for repelling mosquitoes that fits over your belt like a portable
telephone pager and imitates the sound of a dragonfly.

The notion of being seen in my dahlia bed with a
beeperlike instrument on my belt was horrifying when
it occurred to me that people might mistake me for a
lawyer. Rather than see my reputation ruined, I decided
to take the dragonfly ploy a step further.

So I set to work with needle and thread, making
a cotton suit, gossamer wings (actually Saran Wrap
stretched over bent coat hangers), and little sets of
feelers crafted from plastic shoe-stretchers which looked
pretty darn realistic.

Delia's costume matched mine except it was smaller.
After consulting a bug encyclopedia, we realized that
dragonflies by definition have "long slender bodies,"
making them the Jane Fondas of the insect world; since

we have short, chubby bodies, we could only hope that mosquitoes are nearsighted.

At the suggestion of a university professor, we practiced intoning the mantra "ohhhm, ohhhm," because it resembles the sound a dragonfly makes. He noted that, if it didn't repel the mosquitoes, it would certainly attract Buddhists and at least we'd have company.

When we are in our costumes, we feel that we truly personify the concept of dressing for success.

We like to think of our little gambit as life imitating art and, if it works, Delia and I plan to branch out into a line of theme clothing for gardeners who are sick of wearing old dungarees and dirty boots. We'll start with owl suits for vegetable growers and then move on to cat costumes for berry patches in need of an anti-bird patrol.

While our garden guardian suits are generating an initially startled reaction, we think it's only a matter of time before the environmentally conscientious come around.

They will surely agree that, when it comes to defensive gardening, sometimes it pays to go buggy.

In fact, most of us novice growers already are. We're hardcore alarmists: We see a borer in every torn leaf, and a blight in every sun-burned petal. When we're not fretting about bugs, we're agonizing over the fact that there's not enough (or too much) rain, that it's been too hot (or too cold), that the peat moss is promoting fungus.

Since I'm as guilty as anybody, all I can do on behalf of my fellow plant putterers is to plead overenthusiasm. Just as the new mother is convinced that someone is going to drop her baby, we too are certain that the beautiful new flower that has bloomed after months of anticipation is going to fall prey to foraging bugs, a driving rainstorm, or the hand of a thief.

There is something odd in the soul of gardeners, who thrive on all the strife and worry that accompany a hobby whose goal is to produce beauty. Anyone who tells you that gardening is soothing is either lying or old and mellow. After all, it's such a problem-ridden area that the federal government subsidizes a health department and infirmary—the Cooperative Extension Service—to care for those wounded in the line of duty.

I'm still searching for calm among my beds, Saran-gossamer wings spread and an "ohhhm" on my lips.

IF YOU BRING ONE MORE BOUQUET TO WORK, YOU'RE FIRED

When you're not fending off ravenous insects, keeping the birds from soiling your flowers, or worrying if your garden is getting enough water, you can try for the ultimate *coup*: the jealousy of colleagues.

For us late-blooming botanists there is no greater thrill than making up an obscenely overdone bouquet of huge and fragrant blossoms *grown by our very own hands* and taking it to work to be displayed in a prominent place. Personally, I favor the receptionist's desk because its central location assures that nobody can avoid noticing my handiwork.

This, of course, paves the way for outright gifts of bouquets, which cannot be taken lightly as the season progresses and the flowerbeds spit out more lovely blooms than you can ever possibly use on your own.

After every room in my house is filled with multiple arrangements in vases, pots, and baskets, after my neighbors have all been blessed by my largesse, then there's nowhere for me to turn but the workplace, where everyone from secretaries to executives to janitors can be sure that, come nightfall, they too will be trying to drive home without spilling a jar full of water and flowers that is precariously riding on the floor of the car.

In order to get the fullest blossoms to the workplace in a state as near perfection as possible, I have devised a system for culling and arranging. Not only does it make the best use of my time: It gives my neighbors a laugh besides.

After I've taken Delia out for her morning routine, I pull on my high Wellington boots, which I wear with my nightgown and a pair of canvas gloves. Thus garbed in the latest low couture, I go out to the soggy dew-laden yard. Early morning is no time to be fashion-conscious. It's not a good idea to put on one's good office clothes and soft, imported leather shoes before heading out to cut a bouquet. When accidentally jammed into a muddy furrow between rows of plants, most high-heeled pumps do not respond well. Even if you try walking lightly on tiptoes, there's no way to avoid the awful oozing of water and muck around the sole. Before you can say "ninety bucks down the drain," your shoes and stockings are ruined and so is your temper. That's why I stick to boots; it keeps my spirits and Papagallos from sinking.

After I fill my basket—and before I start dressing for work—I've got time for the eye-opening cup of coffee that allows me to see what I've just cut. Noting that peachy-lemon dahlias outnumber any other flower—probably because the variety "Mary Jo" is the heaviest producer in the garden—I realize that my major chal-

"OOOH, MOTTY! THESE ARE BEEYOOTEEFUL!"

lenge will be to utilize all the Mary Jos without making the arrangements tediously alike and more peachy-pink than a row of Pepto-Bismol bottles.

By my second cup of coffee I have things figured out. I'll use most of the Mary Jos to replace withered bouquets that are drooping in my own house. Now the trick is getting the rest to work safely—no spills, no crushed blossoms—in containers that I don't mind giving up.

A rule of etiquette for flower-givers is: Never give a bouquet in a vase you want returned. Since chances are good you'll never see your precious Waterford heirloom again, the best way to avoid angry words with someone who was *certain* you meant her to keep the whole thing—flowers, pitcher, and all—is to use empty food containers such as large mayonnaise or spaghetti sauce jars, or tall, wide-mouthed juice bottles.

There is no danger anybody will want to keep these; that's how I came to have an entire cupboard of them. It's a family tradition. My mother had the world's largest collection of plastic margarine and whipped topping bowls; for me, it's jars.

Once I have my usual half-dozen floral tributes ready to roll, the big question is: How do I get them to work without having the jars break, the water slop out all over the place, and the blossoms smoosh together like college students filling a phone booth to prize-winning capacity?

The answer, I've discovered, is old bath towels and a laundry basket. I take a large, square heavy-duty plastic laundry basket with sturdy handles, place a thick towel in the bottom, and then carefully set individual pots of posies in place, wrapping each in another towel as a buffer.

While it looks as though babies are being bundled up to go out in 20-degree weather, the system *does* work, keeping the flower containers solidly in place, each half-filled with water to avoid spillage in the event that I decide to try for a new land-speed record en route to work.

Once there, I unveil my treasure to much acclaim from my colleagues. Little do they realize that, thus encouraged, I will deluge them with floral tributes until they beg me to stop. I recall walking through the office setting those first vibrantly colorful bouquets on desks, and the flurry of thanks flung my way.

"Oooh, Motty! These are beeyooteeful!" called out a particularly sweet secretary who speaks Rhode Island-ese as a first language.

"Wow! Whatta ya call these?" asked a horticulturally impaired man who is expert about professional sports but whose only experience with things that grow involves mold in sneakers.

"I had no idea you had any sort of talent whatsoever!" drawled the chronically snide office blueblood, whose

Mummy undoubtedly has hordes of gardeners on the estate back home in Watch Hill.

Another valuable lesson I learned early on about presenting vases of flowers is that, if the recipient is on the phone when you set the container on her desk, it's a good idea to be sure she knows it's near her elbow. Nothing takes the joy out of an event faster than the sight of an enraged woman frantically using the hem of her designer blouse to mop up plant water that's soaking through the pages of the company's annual report.

Even under the happiest of circumstances, there are only so many times your closest friends can express cooing admiration for your flowers before their enthusiasm begins to wilt.

By mid-August of my first gardening year, when the entire office had been swamped by the floral deluge and I was reduced to putting bouquets on the desks of people I don't even particularly like, I began to feel like someone who had accessorized her clothing with a garlic necklace.

At the sight of me struggling off the elevator with a basket laden with assorted pots and jars of dahlias, colleagues would pretend to take phone calls or suddenly dash off to the restroom. It became clear that if I pressed one more exquisite collection of garden cuttings on these people, they would arise and fling me from an upper-story window.

I also learned how it feels to have people snarl at the endless bounty of homegrown tomatoes that have been brought to work too many times. Even though I've done my own share of snarling at the vegetable-givers, I was shocked to find that, when it comes to divvying up my flowers, I'm just as bad as they are. I am a wildly overgenerous giver, relentless at getting rid of the harvest. The revelation sickened me but did not prevent my impersonation of the FTD delivery boy.

There's probably nothing worse than the unbridled joy of the amateur gardener who, having achieved success, cannot suppress the desire to preen ever so slightly.

I mean, most of the pinstripe types with whom I share employment in the city are apartment dwellers who have no personal knowledge of peat moss. As an endorsement of life in the suburbs, I thought showing off the fruits of gardening would make converts out of even the most dedicated urbanites. And at first the propaganda seemed to work.

My co-workers initially responded with smiles of delight as I lugged in pots of roses, gladioli, and dahlias. Rather rapidly, it now seems as I look back, they were heartily sick of these exhibitions, which far exceeded their collective PQ (posie quotient). Incredulous expressions such as "These are from *your* garden?" metamorphosed into mutters of "Will these be dying soon?"

At desks all around me, people furtively began to pray for a killing frost.

Even the office wit, a dapper young fellow who imagines himself to be the local David Letterman, was moved to flex his skills.

Surveying the desk tops adorned with brimming vases, he turned slowly and asked, "Congratulations, kiddo. These *are* from your wedding, aren't they?"

As the company's Official Spinster in Residence, I am required to tolerate this sort of repartee. I usually manage to retaliate in my own small way, such as by gluing the offender's coffee cup to the center of his engagement calendar.

I would have thought he'd rather have the flowers.

Meanwhile, I could sympathize with co-workers who were suffering from a floral embarrassment of riches. To be perfectly honest, by the time fall finally arrived I'd about had it with flower cutting and arranging, too—a feeling I was to regret intensely as winter dragged on.

After the first year of bounty, I calmed down and became content to bring a few bouquets into the house and to share some with friends. Occasionally I'll still take pitchers of particularly pretty flowers to work, but I no longer feel obligated to make the place look like a float in the Tournament of Roses parade.

While I needed the ego boost for my first effort, the praise that made all the hard work worthwhile, I have come to learn that the beauty of flowers exists for itself and does not require outside applause—although it *is* nice to surprise someone with a bunch of posies.

The only person who loved each and every bouquet and never failed to phone and say how much they brightened her day was my friend Fran, housebound and terminally ill. No matter how tedious the dahlias became to others who could no longer muster the energy to make approving comments, Fran always proclaimed them to be the best medicine, and I knew she meant it. She knew these were not modern, mass-produced arrangements ordered by phone. My bouquets, overflowing with love and jammed with blooms, were in the tradition of taking homegrown or handmade gifts to the sickroom. In the face of helplessness, it's a time-honored way to offer comfort. When cures elude, a simple gift of beauty must do.

To me, the act of showing off my flowers in the office was merely a glimpse into *my* secret life as a hobbyist. Among my colleagues, who include closet watercolor painters, frustrated concert pianists, and dedicated Saturday morning long-distance hikers, I believe I can take my rightful place as a "secret gardener" whose novice status will always be—like their own pursuits—merely a passionate hobby. To me, showing off my flowers is something done in lieu of displaying children's photos or bowling trophies or dance contest ribbons.

And, considering the cellulite factor, it's a lot less harmful than the handiwork of the office cohort whose hobby is baking. From the viewpoint of the chronic dieter, there are no words too strong for this person, who lives to fiddle with semisweet chocolate and sugar.

Who could possibly forgive—or resist—the presentation of double-fudge brownies with chopped nuts, piping hot cinnamon coffee cake with enough calories to fuel a professional basketball team, a spectacular multidecker torte that was baked as a predinner party experiment?

Show me an office with a baking hobbyist and I will show you a roomful of people who are doing extra sit-ups and skipping lunch on a regular basis. That's because it's not enough for bakers to bake; they have to wave their aromatic creations under your nose and beseech you to try just a teensy-weensy piece.

Sure. How about a crumb the size of, say, Manhattan?

There's just no escaping. But at least my flowers aren't fattening.

Without question my boldest move gift-wise was when I offered to do all the flower arrangements for a wedding reception. Two hundred guests were being received at the newlyweds' home, widely acknowledged by the rest of us who live here as the nicest house in the neighborhood. It is a modern palace on the waterfront, overlooking three acres of salt marsh and the Atlantic Ocean. Guests would be meandering between a hot buffet indoors and a bar set up on the lawn to catch the sea breeze.

Certainly the flowers would have to be spectacular, and they would need to be artfully arranged. In this setting, nothing second-rate would do. Because the bridegroom was among the first to welcome me to the neighborhood and had always stopped to compliment my flowers, I decided to offer him and his new wife a gift symbolic of the flowering of their love.

It was quite a challenge I set for myself as I picked up the phone, dialed, took a deep breath, and said, "As my gift, I would like to do all the flowers for the reception."

"That'll be great," he said, with real warmth and a touch of surprise in his voice. "Do you think you'll have enough? What about containers?"

I assured him the garden would still be producing madly when the big day arrived, a full two weeks later. Almost as an afterthought, I asked how many bouquets he thought he'd need.

"Probably no more than a couple dozen," he said. "You know: some large ones, some smaller ones for accents. And a really nice *big* centerpiece for the buffet table."

Gulping every so slightly, I told him I thought it

YARROW (CREAM, GOLDEN, YELLOW, AND RED)

would be no problem. Then I hung up and swooned against the kitchen countertop.

"Fine," I muttered to myself. "Now all I have to do is mug a florist."

I went out to the garden and walked around, examining the roses for the dark red leaves that indicate forthcoming buds. I checked to see that the frosty-pink, white and fuchsia yarrow that I like to use in place of baby's breath was still abundant. I took a stroll around the dahlia bed and was relieved to find that, as usual, there were plenty of medium-size blooms.

I was worried, though, about having enough of the giant decorative-style cactus blossoms, which would provide a focal point for the major arrangements. In desperation I sought out John the Dahlia King, who assured me that, should I run short, he'd be glad to contribute some of his own enormous supply. Feeling better, I went inside to inspect the condition of my containers.

Clearly this was a whole different ball game from taking bouquets to work in spaghetti sauce jars. I began assembling my good crystal vases and some heirloom antique china pieces that are of such sentimental value that they seem like old friends.

Regardless of the challenge, I began to feel a glowing sort of confidence about my ability to deliver the goods.

While I had at least five large and attractive

containers—and I was giving the bridal couple a cut-glass vase in seafoam green—I thought it might be nice to use some of their favorite decorative pieces. One evening I went to the house and asked if there were any pitchers or porcelain urns they'd like me to use.

They immediately offered a pair of lovely lead crystal bud vases for each end of a serving table and a wonderful old piece of luminescent white lusterware that had belonged to the bridegroom's late mother.

"Do you think you might use this?" he asked, an oddly gruff tone in his voice. "Maybe you could put in some of those big red flowers I like so much." He referred to the outrageously overblown Red Rocket dahlias whose feathery blooms look like the hats of Las Vegas showgirls.

"I think they'd be perfect with some softer small white flowers," I replied. "Maybe some spider mums, a few of the red-and-lemon roses, that sort of thing."

"Well, you decide," he said, clearing his throat suspiciously and looking pleased.

As the plans progressed, the couple slipped increasingly into the spirit of things. They began to see that their flowers were being custom-designed by someone who genuinely wanted to share their happiness and make the decorations a meaningful part of their special day.

On the morning of the affair, which was to begin at 2 P.M., I was up at the crack of dawn, cutting every blossom in sight and foraging among the frothy wildflowers I'd planted from seed in the vacant lot next door. The harvest yielded my own silver artemesia, yarrow, baby's breath, five shades of roses, a dozen varieties and colors of dahlia, mums in lavender and bronze, and ruby canna lily plumes. The wildflowers included daisies, Queen Anne's lace, and sprigs of bittersweet.

For good measure, John the Dahlia King volunteered sensational pure white cactus dahlias as well as smaller varieties in delicate pastel shades that seemed representations of the hope and fragility of two lives joining.

By the time I'd filled three large baskets with cut flowers, the sun was blazing. It was a day filled with glorious promise. I breathed a silent prayer that I'd be able to do my part to make it special—and that I wouldn't suddenly become all thumbs, overwhelmed by the enormity of the task I'd so enthusiastically undertaken.

As it turned out, my natural instinct for organization (I'm an incorrigible list-maker and check-marker of jobs done) kicked in and helped keep me focused. After shooing the pets into the backyard, I rolled up my sleeves and began to prepare my floral-arrangement assembly line.

The entire kitchen was filled with flowers that needed to be sorted for height, color, and showiness. Some spectacular blooms were obvious candidates for starring roles in arrangements—the hot-pink cactus dahlias, the satiny-perfect Peace rose—while others, more compact in size and soft in color, were destined to be supporting players.

As I stood knee-deep in beautiful blossoms, casting my eye over the vases and deciding which were suited for certain flowers and where they'd look best, I felt as though I had finally overdosed on my hobby: I was as deliriously joyful as a chocoholic who finds herself accidently trapped overnight in a Fanny Farmer factory.

What a sweet frenzy of indecision I enjoyed! First I tried all-white combinations of flower textures, thinking how they symbolized the freshness of newly pledged love. Then I experimented with whimsical, airy Victorian sprays of pale pink roses and baby's breath, knowing they'd be an ideal match for the bride's gown, a turn-of-the-century confection of champagne-colored lace. Because her hair is a burnished copper-red, I did two huge bouquets that were tributes to a golden girl: bronze mums and spikey cactus dahlias, Queen Anne's lace, creamy yellow snapdragons, and the lush salmon-peach Tropicana rose.

Last of all, whispering the private wish, "Bring them

luck," I placed the Red Rocket dahlias in the white lusterware vase that had been the groom's mother's when she was a young bride.

By noon there were nineteen flower arrangements lined up on my kitchen countertops, and I was wondering how in the world I'd ever get them to their final destination. I wound up dumping out a huge file drawer of papers and using that as an impromptu packing crate, supplementing my usual laundry baskets and several big buckets.

Clutching the bottom of the containers to be sure they held secure, I edged my way to the car, filling the backseat, passenger seat, and floor. Going a steady five miles per hour in first gear, I drove to my neighbor's house and rang the bell.

The bride, in her floating Victorian gown, answered the door.

"Oh, Martha," she said, "they're gorgeous."

While the caterer and his drill-team band of employees set up warming pans and platters of iced shellfish, and arranged tables covered in snow-white cloths, I carried in the flower arrangements, trying not to get in the way.

"Will it be all right if I put this here?" I asked.

"I'm afraid we might knock it over," he replied. "If you set it under the table, we'll put it in place after we've got all the serving pieces laid out." I decided to wait.

While I changed my mind at least a dozen times about where various colors and sizes of arrangements would be suitable, I finally got everything in place.

I put smaller bouquets on the end tables; the matching crystal bud vases full of fragrant roses occupied each end of the buffet table. A huge bowl filled to capacity with vibrant blossoms was the centerpiece for the table where the bride's family would sit. The all white arrangement commanded the entry-hall table where the guest register was placed.

The antique lusterware vase, the bridegroom decided, would go at the head table.

I went home to change into my party clothes with little time to spare. When I returned, the caterer had done his job and the aroma of seafood, exotic cheeses, caviar, and pungent sauces mingled with the delicate fragrance of roses. Because I knew no one but the bride and groom, I took a chair in the corner.

Soon the groom was standing before me with an elderly man who, except for the extra character lines and some gray in his dark hair, looked remarkably like him.

"This is my father," he said, as I stood up and took the older man's hand. "This is Martha, my neighbor. She grew all these beautiful flowers."

"Did you make these arrangements, too?" he asked.

"Yes," I said. "I've never done anything quite like it

before. I'm not a professional, so I hope they're all right."

As he looked at the lusterware vase that had been his wife's, his smile nearly outshone the porcelain.

"Eat your heart out, FTD," I thought.

FLOWER SHOWS
ARE NOT FOR WIMPS

My palms are sweating, and my stomach feels as though an entire troupe of Russian bears are using it for somersault practice.

What's going on? Am I waiting to win the lottery? Expecting to receive nomination for the Pulitzer Prize? Steeling up for dental surgery?

Much worse. I am entering my first flower show.

My ears still ringing from the praise my arrangements have received at the wedding reception, I have thrown caution to the wind and have entered the big-time arena. I, who a few short years ago knew nothing about dahlias, am now a contestant in the Rhode Island Dahlia Society's annual show.

This is the equivalent of putting your best peanut-butter-and-jelly sandwich up against one of Julia Child's gourmet meals.

The Dahlia Society has been putting on a show the weekend after Labor Day for twenty-five years. Because the group is part of the American Dahlia Society and the North Atlantic Conference, its show can attract as many as 500 entries. While it's fun to beat members of such prestigious clubs as the Long Island Dahlia Society, local growers insist the most important thing is simply to go one-on-one against another grower, no matter where he or she is from.

Besides winning ribbons and trophies another goal of dahlia growers is to score high with new varieties they've developed—seedlings not previously judged. If one of these scores eighty-five or ninety, a grower can put it on the market and get as much as twenty-five dollars per tuber.

I had attended the state dahlia show the year before to see what it was all about and was dumbstruck by the rows of tables filled with cone-shaped containers, each holding a single stem—some with multiple blossoms. There were dahlias of every shape and size, some so enormous they sat on the floor, looking like tropical trees.

In a separate room, off the main judging area, were floral arrangements awarded ribbons by a committee of the garden club. I looked them over carefully, laughed, and said to a friend, "I could do better than that!"

I would live to eat these words.

The very next year, during the week before the show, I wandered next door to watch John the Dahlia King making last-minute decisions about which blooms he would enter. He was walking up his rows, examining plants and making notes.

"How do you know which one is a winner?" I asked, since they all looked terrific to me.

"You see this one here?" he asked, pointing with his pencil to a soft lavender cactus dahlia. "Now look at this one."

He pointed to a blossom that, to me, looked identical.

"The first one's a winner and the second one isn't," he explained.

"I don't understand," I said. "They're both beautiful."

"The first one's got foliage with five leaves on both sides of the stem. The second has five leaves on one side and four on the other. It would be judged lower."

While, at the time, I gave him a dumb stare of disbelief, I should have considered this description of the minutiae of judging a warning sign. I wasn't getting the message that flower shows are not for wimps. When it comes to confidence in gardening, I am Wimp of the Western World.

Nonetheless I couldn't resist a slight blush of pride when John said, "You've had several nice specimens this year. Why don't you give it a try?"

"Me?" I asked. "The dahlia show? I don't think I'm ready for *that* yet."

"You'll never know till you get your feet wet," he said. "Let's go take a look."

The next thing I knew we were in *my* dahlia bed and I was wringing my hands as John scrutinized first one, then another blossom.

"You should have pinched this one back," he said, disapprovingly. "You've got a nice flower but there's no foliage."

"What about this one?" I asked, pointing to a favorite burgundy ball dahlia.

He looked at me as though I couldn't possibly be serious and moved down the row without bothering to answer.

"Now *here's* a nice one," he said, pouncing on a small purple cactus that, while a nice, rich color, seemed fairly ordinary to me. "What's the name?" he asked.

"I'm not sure," I confessed. "I lost the tag."

John issued one of those deep sighs that people practice when they're silently counting to ten.

"You've got to keep the tags straight," he said for what was probably the fortieth time since I'd known him. "Make a list of what you've planted."

He was about to give up on me when I said those fateful words I would live to regret. "Maybe," I suggested, "I could try entering the floral arrangement category. It wouldn't be as though the whole thing rode on a single flower. And I love making up bouquets."

"Well, go ahead," he said. "At least you'll get an idea of what the show's like."

Everybody there was friendly, he assured me, and would treat me gently.

When it comes to deciding that plants aren't up to

snuff, the kindly old growers are merciless. It took but a single show to determine that I make an excellent spectator but a pathetic contestant.

But before I knew about life in the trenches, I spent an entire week planning my prize-winning floral arrangement. After all, how could I lose? My garden had never looked better and total strangers had raved about my lovely bouquets. It was a sure thing.

John brought home a copy of the show's program listing the various categories. I found that one floral arrangement division required that the flowers be displayed in an antique kitchen implement. "Just the thing!" I thought, since I had many well-worn utensils I'd saved from my mother's house. Rummaging around in the cabinets under the sink, I found a grand old footed collander.

All week long I fussed over my purple-and-white variegated dahlias, knowing I wanted them to star in the entry, with support from soft lavender, pink, and white blooms. Each night I would check to see if the flowers were opening on schedule. If any expanded too soon, the center would be "blown." Such an explosion of the core into yellow pollen automatically disqualifies the entire entry.

By the time I'd finished my first cup of coffee on the morning of the show, I was already a nervous wreck. John, meanwhile, had been up at 3 A.M., using a flashlight to see which flowers to cut. As I went through my dew-heavy dahlias, none seemed good enough.

"Phooey!" I muttered, stamping my foot like a petulant teenager. I did, in fact, feel like an awkward and uncertain adolescent, preparing to give a piano recital with one hand in a cast.

"I'm not even there yet and I already hate the dahlia show," I shouted across the fence to John. "This is all your fault!" He laughed merrily and went about the business of packing the blooms in buckets of water and tall, supportive bottles that filled his truck.

When at last I was satisfied with my basketful of blooms, I took them up to the kitchen to begin arranging. As I attempted to collect the flowers artistically in the clear glass bowl lining the collander, they took turns falling over, shedding their leaves and magically appearing either too tall or too short. After a prolonged period of fussing over an arrangement that, normally, I could execute blindfolded in five minutes, I heaved a sigh of resignation, wrapped everything in shock-absorbing towels and packed it in the car.

I had an hour to drive to the show hall, twelve miles away, and get myself registered and my arrangement properly tagged. By 10 A.M. the doors would be closed and locked, and exhibitors shooed away so eight teams of judges, three to a team, could go about their precise, meticulous work. I would later learn that a gorgeous bloom had been disqualified because one leaf of its green foliage contained a single tiny brown spot!

Driving at a snail's pace and cringing at every bump, I made my way to the exhibition hall where clusters of wizened men were grouped, disputing the proper classification of a new species. Cars and trucks bearing license plates from three states were backed up with trunks open and tailgates down. A steady stream of men and women moved between the vehicles and the show hall, carrying containers of blossoms.

Overcome with excitement and awe, I felt I was experiencing the ultimate gardener's thrill: a chance to hobnob with legendary growers. I also felt totally unworthy in the presence of these esteemed gardeners, and so looked around for my human security blanket, John. I spotted him, peering into the back of his panel truck, jammed with buckets of flowers. He was trying to get organized and start "staging"—the technical term for supporting the stem with a small wooden stake and turning the bloom to face a certain direction with two sets of foliage showing.

This didn't prevent me from approaching him for solace. He didn't exactly say, "Scram, kid; you're bothering me," but I could see he was too busy to hold my hand. I asked him to point out Bill Dykstra, one of the dahlia world's most renowned propagators of new varieties.

"He's the gray-haired fellow," said John helpfully.

I looked around and noted that, without exception, everybody in the place had gray hair, including John.

It turns out that many folks on the show circuit, those who travel to exhibitions within their own conference area, are retired. One elderly man from Massachusetts averages a show each weekend, packing his car and driving to auditoriums all over the East Coast.

At the show hall, I looked at the local dahlia growers, a collection of exotic personalities with blooms to match. There were husband-and-wife teams in denims and sneakers, setting up their exhibits with the efficiency of years of practice. There was a large man in coveralls who engaged anyone who'd stop to argue the heated topic of what he believed were incorrect classification numbers. It all sounded like double Dutch to a novice like me.

In the cool darkness of the hall, I passed knots of men all wearing khaki and baseball caps advertising various dahlia clubs or farm equipment. Sitting at the registration table, her own flowers already neatly placed on the long rows of tables covered with white paper cloths, was a woman wearing a cotton skirt, a flowered blouse, and an enormous straw hat. A fluffy Pekinese sat quietly at her side.

"Yes, my dear?" the registrar prompted me. "Do you have something you'd like to enter?"

"I have a flower arrangement," I said, uncertainly. "What do I do?"

"Just sign your name right here in the register," she said, handing me a tag that was to be placed—with my name discreetly folded inside—under the front edge of my container. Later the judges would write comments on the slip of paper and, perhaps, affix a ribbon!

The sight of the official entry tags and a list of rules as thick as the Congressional Record was enough to turn my entire body into a mass of quivering Jell-O.

Gulping, I signed in and headed to the anteroom, where floral arrangements were to be displayed separately from the individual blooms fighting it out in myriad categories of size and classification. (Serious dahlia growers, who focus exclusively on the quality of single blossoms, don't even consider flower arranging a real category. To them, it's the equivalent of the Miss Congeniality award in the Miss America pageant.)

As I approached the flower arranging area, I passed the Court of Honor, a multitiered showcase draped with white linen—empty now but awaiting the grand winners who would be judged best of the best and displayed at the front. In a late-afternoon ceremony their growers would be called forward and, amid much applause, given trophies and cash awards.

Once inside the display room, I found little cause for optimism. It seemed to me that every other entry had been professionally done. All had a sleek look of perfection while my riotous and cluttered bouquet appeared gauche by comparison, as though a Kmart production had accidentally wound up in Saks Fifth Avenue. In my category, the one featuring antique kitchen implements, my biased opinion was that the other props looked like reproductions. I told myself that the blowsy, exuberant feel of my arrangement was perfect for the venerable double-handled collander that held it.

Still, I felt dispirited as I filled out my entry tags, fluffed up my greenery, and affected the frozen smile of someone who has just watched her date dance off in the arms of the prom queen. Ordeal over, I went home to my garden, where I reassured the flowers that they were *all* winners as far as I was concerned. Being ridiculously overproud of my dahlias, I secretly admitted that, if their beauty was not acknowledged with some sort of ribbon, I would be crushed like yesterday's boutonniere.

It was not to be.

John phoned later to gently tell me it had been a slaughter.

"I heard the judges say they thought you had too many nice blooms," he said, trying to cheer me up. "They tended to go toward the sparser arrangements that were more formal."

While my effort was being dismissed as excessive,

John had reeled in fifty-five ribbons and seven spots in the supreme Court of Honor.

Although he speaks with maddening nonchalance about his hard-won ribbons ("I just throw 'em in a box"), he's still as eager to test the mettle of his petals as he was twenty years ago.

I, on the other hand, do not have the right stuff for flower competition. My feelings had been hurt! After sulking around the house for twenty-four hours, I decided the whole thing had been a valuable lesson because I had learned my place: It is in the peace and quiet of my flowerbeds, gardening for my own pleasure.

The thrill of victory in competition could not offer a greater reward because any time I can get *anything* to respond with blooms, I feel I've won a prize. Certainly no ribbon is brighter than a room full of flowers you've grown yourself.

There is, however, a place for the proud amateur gardener who likes others to appreciate and recognize his skills—and it's not at a high-stakes specialty flower show. It's either in a mixed-variety contest or that oldest and homiest of arenas, the county fair. There is a world of difference in these competitions. The dahlia show, for instance, where I got my baptism of fire, is at the top end of the scale. There, only one kind of flower is featured, and the categories are so detailed and confusing that the average visitor doesn't understand much of what he sees.

Besides the dahlia show, societies of enthusiasts hold similar contests for the growers of roses, gladioli, begonias, azaleas and rhododendrons, chrysanthemums, daylilies, and many others. Wherever there is a club of people avid about one particular flower, you will find a show. You will also find a lot of folks who believe that any flower other than their own is a weed.

In shows held by these groups, you find a fastidiousness with detail and an entire language of growing that takes years of study to absorb. Who could possibly master in a short time the seventy-five classes of dahlias in fifteen colors? All you can hope for is a vague understanding that classes have something to do with size and type.

Even master propagators, eager to show off a variety that's so new it has only a number, have had their breakthrough work dismissed as inferior—only to return the next year with a hardier specimen. Serious growers *never* get their feelings hurt, although they may get mad if they feel the judging was weighted toward a particular style of presentation. To them, there's always another show.

Amateurs with easily wounded pride are better off trying their luck at a fair that exists for fun rather than serious competition.

You won't find a bigger selection of categories or throngs of happier participants than at a county fair, where even kids are encouraged to strut their stuff.

"The judging is not as close," says John, who notes that these events are usually monitored by someone with more general expertise, like a university professor of horticulture.

The fun of a county fair, peopled by what John calls Grange types, is in the diversity. A roomful of high-quality dahlias is an imposing sight, but I prefer someone's prize-winning pumpkin or homemade quilt. At a county fair everyone from 4-H Club youngsters to great-grandmothers get into the act, exhibiting not only plants and flowers but lovingly crafted ceramics, hand-crocheted tablecloths, knitted sweaters, fresh-baked breads and desserts made from recipes, not boxed mixes, and home-canned relish, jams, and jellies.

When I was a kid we faithfully attended the county fair. I spent my time there whining for baby animals, including goats, lambs, and calves that we had no space for at home. My mother, who held a black belt in baking, was compelled to look closely at the dessert competition and declare that the piecrusts looked a little overdone. She never ceased to exclaim, however, over the height and perfection of the homemade bread—the only thing she was unable to master no matter how many times she tried.

My father spent his time marveling at the size of the squash and the enormous pumpkins, although he was never uncharitable enough to point out that his own garden could easily give the winners a run for their money.

While my parents enjoyed looking at what other people had entered in the show, it never occurred to them to put their own skills on display, since that would be boastful.

In the final analysis, I guess I'm more like my folks than I thought—eager to cheer someone's skills but uncomfortable about showing off my own.

That doesn't mean I'll ever miss a dahlia show. For sheer spectacle, you can't beat it. As long as other growers' blooms are on the line and it's their stomachs, not mine, that contain the frolicking troupe of Russian bears.

THE COMPLEAT
GARDENING
QUIZ

Now that we have progressed this far in the tale of one woman's descent into gardening madness, it seems appropriate to review all we have learned and to introduce some of the bizarre concepts and terms you will be using in your own gardening ventures.

There is, certainly, a language barrier to be overcome when you take up this hobby. Experts will tell you such things as, "You'll need two to four pounds of a 5–10–5 per 100 square feet for your small evergreens," and you will nod knowingly—even though you have no idea what they've just said. If someone talks about "crowns," you think British royalty is being discussed; if "nipping" is suggested, you mistakenly imagine this has something to do with drinking on the job. While a worthy idea, this is not what is meant, at least in gardening jargon.

I have created the following quiz and trivia exam not only to be informative but to show what happens to the average mind when it is subjected to the stresses of life in the green lane.

Remember: There are no winners here, only survivors. Pens ready? Begin.

1. Acid is:
   a. Something Timothy Leary used to recommend dropping.
   b. What your stomach is full of after a big Mexican dinner.
   c. A condition existing when the soil lacks lime.
2. Alkaline is:
   a. A famous baseball player.
   b. An emergency phone service for people troubled by drinking.
   c. "Sweet" soil containing lime or chalk.
3. The definition of "annual" is:
   a. How often most unmarried women over thirty have dates.
   b. When many people balance their checkbooks.
   c. A plant that flowers within a year then dies, like some modern romances.
4. Axil is:
   a. What broke when you overloaded the wheelbarrow.
   b. Someone who behaves as though sick, as in "Fred axil."
   c. The angle between the leaf stalks and stem.
5. The best method of eliminating garden pests is:
   a. Employing a large bouncer.
   b. Moving to a new address.
   c. Using traps, lures, preventative planting, and,

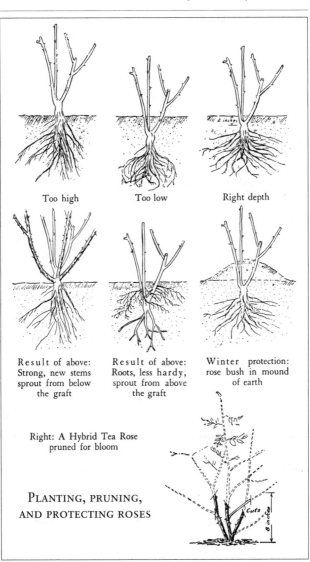

Too high

Too low

Right depth

Result of above: Strong, new stems sprout from below the graft

Result of above: Roots, less hardy, sprout from above the graft

Winter protection: rose bush in mound of earth

Right: A Hybrid Tea Rose pruned for bloom

PLANTING, PRUNING, AND PROTECTING ROSES

in moderation, dusting or spraying with insecticides.

6. Tendril is:
   a. From an Elvis Tune, *Love Me Tendril*.
   b. From a famous novel, *Tendril Is the Night*.
   c. A twining appendage used for support by some climbing plants.

7. Bi-colored is:
   a. What you should do if you can't decide between purchasing the plain or patterned toilet tissue.
   b. How to describe the back of your neck after bending over in the garden for an hour in the noonday sun.
   c. Having two colors on the same petal.

8. True or false? Lily of the Valley is a California girl who like, you know, uh, grows wicked awesome flowers and thinks weeds are grotty.

9. When trimming roses you should always:
   a. Make an advance deposit at the blood bank.
   b. Hire a neighborhood kid you don't like.
   c. Wear stout gloves and body armor.

10. Bud is:
    a. A regular guy.
    b. A regular beer.
    c. A small swelling on a plant from which a leaf or flower grows.

11. A rake is defined as:
    a. Someone you won't attract smelling of Ben-Gay.
    b. What they call a car crash down South, as in "Bubba Billy Joe Jim-Bob got hurt in a rake."
    c. A garden tool with long handle and teeth at the end, good for administering a concussion.

12. Evergreen is:
    a. The color of your eyes when you gaze upon someone else's prize dahlias.
    b. The condition of the hardware store owner's wallet.
    c. Having green foliage throughout the year.
    d. All of the above.

13. Use the word "anemone" in a sentence as in: "He never had anemone in the world."

14. A Dutch hoe is:
    a. A lady of the evening in Amsterdam.
    b. What Santa says, in triplicate, in Holland.
    c. A cultivating tool with a long handle and a flat blade.

15. Grafting is defined as:
    a. What politicians do when they run short of cash.
    b. Cultural payoffs, known as arts and grafts.
    c. Plant propagation using lengths of stem.

16. The most important step in spring planting is:

    a. Soil preparation.

    b. Martini preparation.

    c. Preparation H.

17. Hybrid is:

    a. The opposite of lobrid.

    b. How plants greet each other.

    c. Plant resulting from crossing two distinctly different species.

18. True or false? Burpee's is an embarrassing social problem afflicting gardeners.

19. Aster is defined as:

    a. What the groom did when he proposed to the bride.

    b. The last name of the famous rich guy John Jacob.

    c. A white, purple, or pink daisylike flower.

20. Humus is defined as:

    a. Amusing or funny.

    b. When the air is moist and muggy and you wake up covered with mildew.

    c. Well-rotted organic matter.

21. True or false? Aloe is a friendly greeting exchanged by neighborhood gardeners.

22. An automatic sprinkler system is good for:

    a. Ruining your shoes.

    b. Scaring the cat.

    c. Surprising unwanted guests.

    d. Maintaining moisture even if you're not home to man the hose.

    e. All of the above.

23. Oregano is defined as:

    a. A spice commonly found in Italian cooking.

    b. The Italian equivalent of Japanese paper-folding art.

    c. What you say if someone asks you to move to Portland. (Oregon? No.)

24. A deadhead:

    a. Perfectly describes your last date.

    b. Perfectly describes your last boss.

    c. Perfectly describes the last crumbled bits of a blossom.

25. Leaflets are:

    a. Things with which you're inundated during an election.

    b. The extra section of a tiny dining table.

    c. Each segment of a compound leaf.

26. True or false? The word "phlox" alludes to a Biblical passage in which shepherds abiding in the field were keeping watch by night.

27. Separating is:

    a. A method of dividing crowded plants.

    b. Something that Liz Taylor specializes in.

    c. What your shoulder does from your body after too much digging.

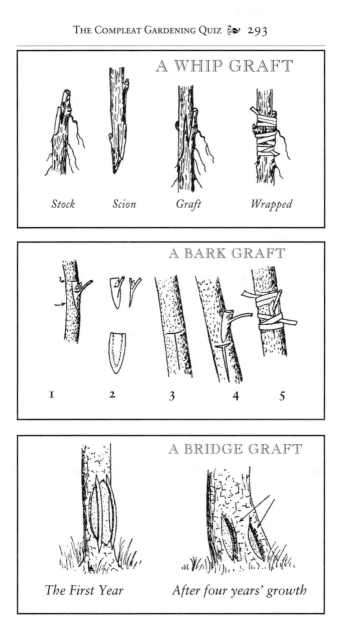

A WHIP GRAFT

Stock *Scion* *Graft* *Wrapped*

A BARK GRAFT

I 2 3 4 5

A BRIDGE GRAFT

The First Year *After four years' growth*

28. Edging is:
    a. How you leave the room after committing a faux pas.
    b. What Cockneys do with their bets.
    c. What you do around the flowerbeds to lend an air of formality while keeping grass at bay.

29. An aphid is:
    a. The phid that comes before the b-phid.
    b. Someone who is intense, as in "Harry's an aphid golfer."
    c. A mite that attacks plants.

30. When applying natural fertilizer you should:
    a. Make sure the cow is done with it.
    b. Never stand downwind.
    c. Postpone spreading it until after your formal garden party.

31. Stamen is:
    a. When a roomful of spinsters wish the males would do.
    b. The fellows who sew stays into foundation garments.
    c. The pollen-producing reproductive organ of a flower.

32. When buying plants the most important thing is:
    a. Your available space.
    b. Your available credit.

    c. The availability of someone else to tend them.

33. Mosses:
    a. The man who parted the Red Sea.
    b. The plural of moose.
    c. Small green bryophytes that form a dense matlike growth.

34. When staking you should always:
    a. Make sure your guest in the black cape really *is* a vampire.
    b. Make sure the gas grill is turned on.
    c. Make sure someone else holds the stick while you wield the hammer.

35. True or false? Pruning is a natural way to relieve the distress of irregularity.

36. The most important thing about your tools is:
    a. Remembering who you loaned them to.
    b. Remembering who you borrowed them from.
    c. Remembering in the spring where you left them in the fall.

37. Picket is:
    a. An unhappy laborer carrying a sign and refusing to work.
    b. What you long to do to another gardener's prize bloom.
    c. A lethal type of decorative fencing.

38. True or false? Gypsy moths are itinerant insects traveling the country in caravans, playing mandolins, and offering to mend your pots and pans and tell your fortune.

39. Marigold is:
    a. To wed a mining heir.
    b. Cheerful bullion.
    c. A popular annual that comes in a yellow or orange color.

40. True or false? "Begonia!" is what an angry Irishman says when he dismisses you.

41. Hosta is:
    a. A belligerent attitude.
    b. A missing labor leader named Jimmy.
    c. A lush perennial with abundant green foliage and tiny lavender blossoms atop tall, erect stems.

42. Cosmos:
    a. The place where Carl Sagan saw billions and billions of stars.
    b. A collection of Helen Gurley Brown's magazine.
    c. A daisylike annual.

43. True or false? Coreopsis is a medical procedure for removing the center of an apple.

44. Poplar is:
    a. What you never were in high school.

    b. The father of the famous actor Bert Lahr.

    c. A slender tree with triangular leaves and light-colored wood.

45. True or false? Wildflowers are plants that like to dress up in leather jackets, ride motorcycles, and hang around with a bad crowd.

46. Fern is:

    a. Not American, as in: "I won't buy a fern car."

    b. The type of bar favored by the chronically trendy.

    c. A flowerless, seedless green plant with divided leaflets.

47. True or false? Catalogue describes two things you'll find by the fireplace on a cold winter night.

48. True or false? Crown vetch is the act of bringing the queen her formal hat.

49. Use the word "weed" in a sentence, such as: "We'd like to stay to dinner but this is Harry's bowling night."

50. True or false? Wisteria is the condition you're in after completing spring planting . . . and after finishing this test.

Think of this exercise as a kind of weedkiller to be used on the crabgrass of life.

PLANT AN AZALEA GARDEN
AND LIVE TO BE 100

It was a sparkling Sunday afternoon in May as I inched along the two-lane country road in front of the Kinney house. Cars were parked on both sides for a mile in each direction, making travel difficult and finding a parking space nearly impossible. Finally, nearly three-quarters of a mile away, I was able to squeeze my car onto a shaded patch of grass. It was quite a trek but well worth it.

I was attending the Azalea Tea Party, for forty years one of southern Rhode Island's best-loved rites of spring. Had I not boldly asked Lorenzo F. Kinney, Jr., for an invitation I would likely have joined the other gate-crashers who are as graciously welcomed into the Kinney gardens as old family friends.

"The garden's always open to the public except on the day of the tea," Kinney explained on the occasion of my visit. "That's by invitation only, but if anybody stops by and asks to come in we always say yes."

Thank goodness. There is almost nothing I wouldn't do to wangle my way into a flower viewing, and the azalea gardens in full cry are a spectacle nonpareil, a glorious celebration of nature and of one grand old man's vision.

Behind the colonial house the Kinneys built in 1927 is a blazing forest comprising four-and-a-half acres of vermillion, white, lavender, plum, shell pink, coral, and salmon.

It is a floral palette that Kinney—the Johnny Appleseed of azaleas for those who savor their local folklore—nurtured for more than sixty years.

For the tea, he was formally attired in a natty gray suit, white shirt, and a red paisley tie, bustling about greeting visitors. While his wife, Elizabeth, stayed indoors where family members were serving tea and goodies, Kinney welcomed every guest, posing for pictures with many.

I stood beside him, a fiery wall of giant azaleas behind us, as a friend captured this moment in the lifetime of a garden that botanical experts predicted would never grow. To me, Lorenzo Kinney, at that time age 95, was an inspiration, as spry and keen as he was eighty years ago.

The tea party is an example of his astonishing exuberance. When he was not posing for others' photos, he was taking his own, nimbly trotting around to position little girls wearing long, lace-trimmed pastel dresses and straw hats in front of the perfect shade of blossom to set off their costumes. He was behaving as if he was relishing a grand new experience, as though he didn't already have thousands of color slides of his flowers

AZALEA: 1 ROOTED CUTTING, 2 PLANT (PINCHED OR
GRAFTED), 3 PLANT FED AND TRIMMED, 4 FLOWERING

stacked in his living room, as though he couldn't imagine a more wonderful thing to do than show his gardens off just one more time.

"So nice to see you here!" he said, beaming and taking the hands of a young couple who had driven a long way for the occasion. Gesturing toward the twin trails winding off into a feathery rainbow, he promised, "You can walk through there the rest of the afternoon and not see everything."

Nothing prepared me for the scale and intensity of areas of azaleas in bloom, some as tall as trees. Like other visitors, I was overwhelmed.

The son of nearby University of Rhode Island's first botany professor, Kinney was inspired by his father and eventually studied agriculture at the university. His Peter Pan-like agelessness was put to good use as he headed the state's 4-H program from 1920 to 1956.

"My father being a botanist, he saw to it that I made collections of weeds and flowers, that I pressed flowers. After he'd been at the university fourteen years, he left to develop a rhododendron nursery with a few azaleas scattered through, so I grew right up with all that exotic color."

The flowers' beauty so captivated him that, when Kinney married in 1927 and built a house on land his father had bought in 1890, he was determined to try his hand at azaleas, taking some of the larger plants from his father's nursery to get started.

"We built this house before we got married," he told me, adding that it was a matter of necessity. "There was no place to go here in Kingston, no rooming houses or anything like that. So we built it and moved right in when we got married. We had just a half-acre lot then, but these fields behind us became available and we gradually acquired them one after another."

Despite Kinney's desire to grow azaleas on his land, he received no encouragement from the experts, who assured him the tender plants would never grow in chilly New England. Lorenzo Kinney didn't believe them.

Despite such warnings, he began planting the small bushes anyhow—shrubs that would grow into giants, some of them forming velvety canopies and long, fiery tunnels of bloom.

"We found the azaleas weren't dying as predicted," he wryly recalled of the first plantings. Moreover, he refused to be limited to the handful of hardy types grown locally and began experimenting with extravagant ornamental shrubs—eventually propagating more than 600 rare varieties. Kinney believed his plants prospered because his low-lying property is shielded by tall evergreens and, therefore, not exposed to the wild, icy winds that rake exposed highlands.

By virtue of his insistence on proving the experts wrong, and because he felt the growing conditions were right, Kinney won a wide reputation for his ability to grow the world's frailest hot-house specimens, including Oriental azaleas, in the bracing New England air.

As much as for the luscious floral display—which participants in a newspaper poll once listed as one of the ten best things about living in this community—it is Lorenzo Kinney's Yankee perseverance that guests and longtime friends celebrate each spring. His determination represents all that is positive about gardening.

In fact, the azalea tea has become a perfect place for many of Kinney's former 4-H youngsters, now middle-aged with grandchildren of their own, to have a reunion. "A great many of them come every year," he said. "They come from as far away as Virginia and Maine.

"Years ago, as a sort of honor, we used to offer a trip to the azalea tea to top young members from around New England, the ones who had demonstrated leadership. We'd only let one carload come in from each state, and we met some very nice young people. We've kept in touch with them through the years."

As one of the more than 500 visitors to tour the

azalea gardens that year, I asked Kinney if he could go out back and point to the oldest plant. There were probably a hundred planted at the same time, some sixty years ago, he said, bursting my romantic bubble of being able to locate the solitary azalea that started the dynasty. He did, however, know precisely which ones those are.

"The ones my father gave us, which were already mature in 1927, are the oldest. We didn't have much land then but, as we got more, we put in so many azaleas that they crowded everything else out. We had a good-size garden with many different flowers but, through the years, the azaleas took over."

Kinney noted that azaleas have been cultivated for centuries and his aim was to toughen them up. "They've been crossed and recrossed so many times we don't know much about the parentage. A good many of them are tender and that's why we started: We wanted to develop more hardy kinds than you find in the South." His wife is from Virginia, a place where azaleas thrive.

Kinney always considered his garden a labora-tory, a place where fragile varieties could be tested until they'd proved their hardiness. As new varieties were unveiled in faraway places, he'd send for some and plant them to learn if they could survive New England's wildly changing climate. He'd wait six years for an answer: By then, if plants were knee-high, he'd know he had another success.

"That's one of the reasons so many people come here to our gardens," he said of the endless testing. "We have so many varieties."

Besides the pink shades prevalent in Florida and the Japanese azaleas imported to South Carolina by wealthy growers, Kinney also sought the extremely delicate Chinese azaleas, desperately wanting to get them established in the North because of their exquisite colors.

"Some of the prettiest ones come from south China where it's real warm," he explained, "and they didn't grow here much until we crossed them with hardier varieties. We started growing the Chinese azaleas and many other kinds that we were advised not to try, and we found that they *did* grow, so we kept adding until now we have some of almost every type. Nearly every inch out back is filled with these azaleas."

A lack of space didn't stop Kinney and his helpers, led by a young woman who was studying for a doctorate in plant science, from planting several thousand azalea seedlings every spring—the busiest season in the garden. As they were planted, some of the mature azaleas were sold off to make room.

In Kinney's garden, where the rainbow range is so striking, keeping the color going is a matter of careful planning. Deciding what new variety to put in each spring and making room to accommodate seedlings is a never-ending challenge. (He pooh-poohed his achievement of ninety-five, noted that a cousin in Florida was 100 and is "way ahead" of him.)

Although the entire color spectrum of azaleas blooms for a few months, he proclaimed, "The middle of May is the best time. We've got lots of color and it's really quite a show." Kinney was so familiar with his beloved garden and so precise in knowing when it looked best that he often insisted visitors come on a specific day so they didn't miss the peak of color of particular azaleas that bloom then quickly fade.

"Azaleas are at their best for not more than a week and if you want to keep your full line of colors and tints right along it takes a lot of plants to do it," he said. "We have a wide range of colors continuously from early May until the end of July. Some flowers are finishing as others are starting. Each variety always blooms at about the same time, so we can plan on early ones, midseason, late midseason, and late. You plant on that schedule and they just come; it goes on naturally. We have as many blooming at one time as another. In the very early spring, there are fewer colors—only the white, a violet, and a pink or red."

Kinney's azaleas begin to flower in early April and some varieties continue until mid-August or even, in some years, into September.

"On any given day," he noted, "we've got one that's the showiest and the others don't look as good, so for that day, that one's your favorite. Our workers, who are mostly college girls, pick out a favorite flower for every day and comment among themselves. Every once in a while we think we've got so many varieties we should discard some of them, but each one has its own characteristic and we generally don't discard it. We keep it because of its bright color or because it grows well."

How they remember the varieties' names—Betty Anne Voss, Nancy of Robinhill, Kennell's Gold—or, for that matter, even choose a single plant from among a sea of brilliance, is anybody's guess.

While he didn't bound down the trails at age ninety-five as he did only a few years before, Kinney went out each day to supervise pruning and transplanting, and to plan for years of future growth.

"I used to guide guests around, but it takes a couple of hours and there are too many other things that need to be done. I tell people to go ahead and walk and, if they want to know anything, just come and ask. We try to have labels on as many plants as possible so people will know what they are, and, of course, all the trails are marked."

On another spring day I dropped by the house, where we sat chatting about the continuing sustenance of gardening. He lead me to his dining room window, where a table was laden with seedlings in pots. There were more upstairs, he said, filling the windows of empty bedrooms.

"We don't have a greenhouse," he explained, "but with the children grown and gone, we can do pretty much what we want inside with plants."

He described how the treasure trove in the windowsills came from cuttings made the previous summer and kept indoors until they're ready for transplant outside. All the seedlings, thousands of them, wouldn't gain maturity for another five years—when Kinney would be 100.

"I probably won't be here to see what they're like," he said, without any note of regret. "But I hope somebody will carry it on."

For a brief moment I reflected on how he was advised to give up the notion of growing azaleas in this dismal climate. I gazed beyond the seedlings, through the window and into the garden, and saw his response—a legacy of beauty bespeaking one man's commitment to a dream.

It seemed to me very likely that Lorenzo Kinney would see these seedlings mature.

Mr. Kinney did, indeed, live to be 100, a milestone that was celebrated at a party in December, 1993, attended by hundreds of friends at his church, Kingston Congregational. He

Lorenzo F. Kinney, Jr.

died the following April. Since then his daughter Betty Faella and her husband have moved into the Kinney home to assure that Mr. Kinney's work continues. His longtime protégée, Sue Gordon, who received her doctorate in plant sciences after presenting a dissertation on bud hardiness in azaleas—a topic chosen by Mr. Kinney—has taken over as curator of the garden.

IT AIN'T OVER 'TIL IT'S OVER:
THE END OF THE SEASON

A garden is a combination trading post, encounter group, social center, and workout class. It can be a place of great serenity and calm or the scene of hot debate. With the asking of one innocuous question, a garden can become a fascinating impromptu classroom where lessons are taught about plant science, growing techniques, and the essentials of life itself.

The garden is the place where I work hardest at the business of being physically and emotionally well. Because I firmly believe that things come into our lives at various times for a specific reason, I am convinced that it was more than coincidence that I took up gardening shortly after I began a long and tedious battle with a cancer-causing virus. I can recall that, on the day I came home from the hospital after surgery, I got out of the car, shook off a friend's helpful arm, and hobbled over to look at my rose bushes. Inhaling the scent, caressing the silken petals was better than any sort of prescription drug.

I have become a passionate midlife gardener, bewitched and utterly enthralled.

In the garden I have relinquished immediacy in favor of mothering along ugly duckling plants which become sensational swans. I am now convinced that life holds no greater fulfillment than watching a flowerbed fill in as plants mature and take shape, its rows blending into each other with their colors and textures weaving a living tapestry. Just as my gardening pals promised, I have come to know that, as long as you have a garden, you're never bored and you're never lonely.

In the garden there is something to cheer about in every season. In my beds, for instance, things appear in a sort of straggling parade: Early spring bulbs offer bits of fresh color that stand out against the brown grass not yet revived; they are quickly followed by azalea, forsythia, and tulips which then give way to the blossoms of summer.

I have even, God help me, learned to appreciate weeding. During these, my first years as a student gardener, I've discovered that I do some of my best thinking while pulling weeds. It's the same sort of mental housekeeping that I once performed while commuting to work, but the tendency to drift into a stupor and shoot past lurking state troopers with radar guns caused me to give that up. I turned to weeding, which had to be done anyhow, as an ideal time for mulling over troublesome issues and coming to grips with annoying situations.

There's something about the mechanics of weeding— the discovery of the Green Thing That Doesn't Belong, the reaching for it, the digging under its roots, the act of wrenching it from the ground—that lets your brain go on automatic pilot and sort through its file of nagging concerns.

If more people took out their frustrations and anger on weeds, there would be less job turnover and fewer instances of domestic violence.

It's better to go out back and yank dandelions out of the petunia patch than to try drop-kicking a surly teenager into the next county. There's nothing like a vigorous stand of pokeweed for taking out your animosity toward the boss. It's amazing how gratifying it can be, after a hard day at the office, to seize a stalk of this stuff and pretend you've got the department head by the throat.

The process of tugging it up by the roots produces the same joyful feeling of victory you'd get from strangling him—without the lengthy prison term. I have noticed that you can grind your teeth and yell, "Take that!" without arousing any suspicion from the neighbors who, if they notice you at all, merely think you've developed a fanatical devotion to the purity of your flowerbed.

People who are desperately in need of weed therapy should not be discouraged if they live in high-rise apartment buildings without the benefit of a terrace garden. My advice is that, if you're driving home from work in a rage because you're doing more and getting paid less than the guy who sits at the next desk, you should pull over to the side of the road and decimate some dogbane. Better still, join with your neighbors and start a community garden in a vacant lot. Share the joy of working off massive bouts of ill temper by going out in teams and eradicating the figwort!

After one of my own frenzied bouts of weeding, I was so pleased with the look of the garden that I decided to give a lawn party and invite all of my gardening buddies to see the fruits of their tutoring.

The flowers were blooming, a soft breeze was blowing, and I was dressed in my prettiest pastel cotton dress. As the guests assembled to sip punch and admire the blossoms, my inherited cat—a brown tabby who is an avid hunter despite consuming two huge meals of expensive canned food each day—put everyone in the party spirit by running up the driveway with a full-grown, obviously dead rabbit in his mouth.

I responded as I believe any well-educated, emotionally stable person would: I shrieked at the top of my lungs. What I yelled wasn't particularly informative since everyone present who wasn't gagging or fainting could see for themselves what the critter du jour was. Nonetheless, I could not stop myself from screaming, "*He's got a rabbit! He's got a rabbit! He's got a rabbit!*"

So much for the tranquility of a summer afternoon

among the flowers—where, incidentally, the cat frequently deposits gifts of deceased field mice, chipmunks, voles, and assorted bird parts. I cannot fully describe how distasteful it is to be digging among the geraniums and suddenly realize I'm touching a cold little mouse foot.

Midsummer brings a frenzy of activity when roses, glads, dahlias, coral bells, lilies, hosta, and bleeding heart all bloom at once. In late fall there are second arrivals of things that blossomed earlier and were pruned to encourage new activity. The dahlias last well into the fall but do not outdistance the chrysanthemums whose fluffy bronze, gold, and lavender heads are the last to bow to cold winds and nipping frost.

By the time the growing season winds down, I think it's safe to say I'm the mellowest person around, having worked myself into a state of blissful exhaustion. I'm sad, though, at the prospect of putting the garden to bed for the winter. The pain is dulled somewhat by the slow pace with which a garden says its long goodbye. Unlike that other joyous time, Christmas, which is over with one big bang, a garden keeps giving its gifts—prolonging the inevitable closing down for winter hibernation.

When the mums are all that's left of the once glorious color, I know that soon the business of tucking the garden away for the winter will be at hand. It's not a time I relish since I know that, unless I catch a plane to

Florida in January for a hibiscus fix, there will be no flowers to fuel my addiction for many months.

Saying goodbye to the garden is a lot like seeing a good friend off on a long journey: You're not sure when you'll be together again and the visit seemed too brief! I have found that to prepare your garden for its winter's sleep is to prepare yourself, too, for the prolonged absence of something you love, something that has been the focus of your life for the happiest months of the year. Because I live in the Northeast, where winters are unpredictable and usually harsh, there's a certain apprehension about what damage may occur during bad weather. More than the cold, I have come to fear the icy winds that blow in off the Atlantic, raking rough hands over the soil and exposing tender roots and bulbs.

So, as part of the farewell ritual, I try to devise ways to assure that the beds and shrubs receive the maximum amount of protection. I feel as if I'm tucking the flowers into a safe, warm bed under a quilt that I've pieced myself—and, to keep out the wind, lashed to the bedposts.

Each autumn I follow a routine that begins with denial: I behave as though by my refusal to prepare the garden for winter I can prevent its arrival. No such luck. The cold hand eventually clamps down, gripping everything in a surprise attack, and I am forced to respond. It usually takes two long weekends in late November to finish all the work.

First I borrow my pal Wimpy's truck and drive to Allie's Feed Store for bales of seedless hay that will prevent soil erosion and keep the ground at an even temperature, thus discouraging the freeze-then-thaw process that can spit buried bulbs out faster than an ejector seat. Then, garbed in heavy gloves that I can no longer do without because: a) it's damn cold and b) the twine holding the bales together would neatly slice through my hands, I lug the bales to the various places they'll be needed. Before the hay can be distributed, though, the flowers themselves must be readied.

First to be dealt with are the gladioli and dahlias, which must be dug up, washed, carefully sorted, and laid out to dry in the chilly sun.

The glads, which go in one pile, are first separated (each bulb has produced at least two new bulbs and, sometimes, a handful of tiny corms), then cleaned and tossed into a common box for storage. To deal with the dahlias—which I don't separate until the following spring—I dig up all plants of a certain variety, wash each in turn by dipping the clumps into a bucket of water, then place them on the walkway to dry. Each is identified by the plant marker I've pulled from the ground and stuck near the clump.

When they're completely dry so they don't rot, a

process which takes a few days, the dahlias are ready to be packed up in the cardboard boxes I've appropriated from helpful liquor store owners. I can testify from personal experience that the sturdiest, most useful dahlia boxes in the world are those that have contained half-gallons of Gallo wine, since they come with cardboard dividers and reinforced bottoms.

I write the name of the dahlia on the outside of the box with a red grease pencil; then I sign "Martha" and circle it. This is a necessity because my dahlias will be transported twelve miles north to spend the winter in the perfect climate of a friend's attic, having a pajama party with his dahlias. Before they are hefted to my car—where they fill the trunk, backseat, and passenger seat so fully that they disrupt my sightline and send zealous cops to their books in search of a moving flower violation—the dahlias are given cozy accommodations.

I cover the bottom of each box with vermiculite, put in the tubers, then cover them completely. Sometimes my friend looks in the boxes, decides he doesn't like what I've done and adds more of *his* vermiculite—and, if I'm lucky, a few stray glad bulbs that he winds up forfeiting in the spring under the age-old "finders-keepers" gardening rule.

I have compared the boxes that he didn't repack with those he did and have found no discernible improvement over my system. But, then, dahlia growers aren't happy unless they're showing you where you went wrong.

Once the dahlias have been subdued, during the first weekend of the fall countdown, I turn to the roses, which must be pruned closely to prevent wind damage from whipping branches. Leaving only a few inches exposed above the crown (the top of the root system), I make a large mound of peat moss and topsoil around the crown, covering all the stem tops. I use my hands to firmly press the soil mixture in place.

Next I go around with my Japanese cutting shears and a heavier pair of pruning blades to cut back the brown stalks of plants that are finished for the year: Hosta, leopard's bane, golden glow, coral bells, lupine, and lilies all must be cut back to encourage nutrients to feed the dormant bulbs and root systems and to prevent wind damage. In places where I've lost soil to erosion in previous years, I pile on an extra layer of the topsoil-peat combination or shredded-leaf mulch.

Then, when just about everything except flowering shrubs is safely shortened to a height of about six inches, I get out my wire-cutters and open the bales of hay. I've found that it takes nearly four bales to lavishly cover three very large beds, a narrow fifty-foot border, and a small space near the house. I discovered three bales were too few after I lost my beloved roses during their first winter by the sea. I learned my lesson and decided to do my utmost to preserve the garden in a way that guarantees years of future joy.

After I've spread the hay, I anchor the whole thing down with commercial fishing net cut and fit specially to each bed. (I measured the beds and cut all the net myself, using a single-blade knife provided by the fisherman who gave me the net. While all my colleagues have homes full of Japanese appliances, I'm certainly the only one with an authentic Japanese fishing net covering my flowerbeds! My friend, John Dykstra—the brother of dahlia propagator Bill Dykstra—kept the net as a sort of prize after he pulled it up from the depths of the Atlantic during a fishing trip.)

Having had the experience—and the blisters—of sawing away for an afternoon, I can imagine it's preferable to chew through a pair of Roy Rogers's old cowboy boots. I'm consoled by the thought that, because of the net's toughness, once it's been sectioned it will give service for a great many winters.

To secure the net I place flat cement blocks and bricks along the exterior borders and use long industrial-strength steel staples at the edges bounded by railroad ties. These I hook through the mesh and hammer solidly into the wood. Once I've made sure the beds are snug, I remove bits of decorative fencing and tidy up, searching for stray tools, balls of string, and discarded plastic plant containers.

The menagerie of tiny animal sculptures—a Scottie, an Airedale puppy, a snoozing cat, three rabbits, and a baby bunny snuggled near its mom—that sit in secret garden spots waiting to surprise and amuse visitors are removed, carefully washed and dried, and brought inside to spend the winter in the all-purpose storage and junk room.

My dog, Delia, is particularly fond of the stone bunnies, being unable to differentiate between them and the real things from a distance. The cat gets in on the act, too, and never fails to stalk the stone Airedale puppy at least once each year. When he discovers his error, he begins to wash his paws in an embarrassed sort of way, hoping nobody has observed his performance.

After all the small tools and garden accessories have been brought inside, I make a quick pass around the stack of wooden pallets outside where I do all my potting, separating, and soil mixing. I gather up opened bags of fertilizer, topsoil, and peat moss for storage in the toolshed, along with plant stakes, revolving sprinkler heads, and buckets.

The wheelbarrow is rinsed out and retired for the season, along with the mower, the weed-whacker, and two garden hoses—one for each side of the house—that must be drained, coiled up and tied, and hung on their pegs.

To protect small ornamental shrubs, I've found that

a burlap wrap keeps wind damage to a minimum. It's also a good idea to perk the shrubs up with an acid-supplement fertilizer in the spring when they're uncovered. When I've got the last shrub swathed, my gardening season has officially ended and I am in need of serious diversion. I find solace in my collection of illustrated gardening books, some of them old and out-of-print, that friends and loved ones like to surprise me with.

I consider the pages filled with photographs of gorgeous, mouth-watering flowerbeds in romantic far-flung places to be inspirational reading on cold nights. The sight of splendidly kept English gardens never fails to elicit a silent vow to work harder at my own beds.

The flowerbeds themselves are a constant reminder of these friends. I need only look at the plants thriving from donated cuttings, bulbs, and tubers to see the faces of those who've shared the joy of gardening with me: The coral bells and bronze mums came from the Neuberts; variegated hosta, St. John's Cross, artemesia, and lemon thyme from the Daniels; bee-balm from Jane; physotegia form Lois Graboys; lavender mums and my favorite pompon dahlias, the dark purple Glen Place, from John the Dahlia King.

This garden with all it contains—plants, sentiment, memories—has become a gift of life to me, filling a void where despair and hopelessness once reigned. As much as I mock my bumbling amateurish efforts and pretend to be cross with those who introduced me to the many faces and personalities of flowers, I am deeply grateful for the joy I've found. As far as I'm concerned, there is nothing more spiritually satisfying than an early morning spent crawling around on my hands and knees, sinking my fingers into the soil and touching something that exists only to be beautiful.

As I have gardened, feeling myself in some sort of deep dialogue with an unseen and silent partner, I have come to know true inner peace. There is no room for hurt, anger, or recriminations in a garden. There is no place for negativity or doubt, no time for self-pity. It is not possible to be unhappy when surrounded by such exquisitely vibrant life.

I have adopted a theory of planting whereby I only choose tiny, tender shrubs and trees, and I always place things far apart in the beds.

The idea is that it will take everything four to six years to mature and my presence will be needed to watch and nurture them. While neighbors order mature ten-foot trees trucked in for instant gratification, I like the thrill that comes from planting fourteen-inch-high seedlings that will gradually be transformed into the widespread wings of a red-twig dogwood, the frilly gingham yellow of a forsythia hedge, the thick fragrance of a lavender border, the musky sweetness of an old-fashioned lilac.

To me, a garden is nature's answer to Las Vegas. There is the dazzling show of flowers unsurpassed by hordes of chorus girls in sequined costumes; the heady sensation of gambling in a high-stakes game where winning is the most fabulous jackpot imaginable and losing is a dire tragedy. If you study the game and are brave, daring, and, perhaps, just a little crazy, you can emerge triumphant.

In the years I've dabbled in the garden, I've been a dedicated student, moderately brave but not terribly daring. Although I'm sometimes not quite sure why things turn out well, I never question success when it comes to flowers. I've taken to heart the most crucial rules of gardening: Read everything, talk to everyone, and never turn down a free plant—the camaraderie is always an extra bonus.

I've learned to be selfish about my time, generous with bouquets, and quick to offer an encouraging word to other novice gardeners. I've learned to tend personal relationships with the same devotion that I lavish on my flowers, believing that all things grow from a loving heart.

And I've learned to never give away my good vases.

THE SEED IS HOPE; THE CROP IS JOY

Chris Davis is beside herself with joy. Outside, in the gardens on the grounds of the Zambarano Unit of the Eleanor Slater State Hospital, is a pepper plant bearing a specimen that's twelve inches long.

Her pepper. The very first thing she has ever grown.

"I'm so excited," she says in tones of pride that remind me of my own childhood experience with Conan the Cucumber.

Chris, a handsome woman who takes great pride in her appearance, always wearing soft makeup and clothing in shades of her favorite purple, has multiple sclerosis. She's been confined to a wheelchair for quite some time now but she has found a perfect outlet for the pent-up creativity that previously found its outlet in eyeshadow and earrings.

Now she's growing eggplant and peppers and planning how to glaze and decorate the pottery dinnerware being made to hold the bounty of the Zambarano garden. This year she became a member of what is surely the most extraordinary garden club in New England, if not the entire country. She has joined the hospital's horticultural therapy group, twenty strong, who have been growing championship vegetables and gorgeous flowers since 1992.

What they are doing at Zambarano, under the leadership of senior gardener Peter Neff and clinical psychologist Barbara Waterman, is nothing short of magical. When I first saw the three-acre paradise, in 1994, I thought it was unlike anything I'd ever seen. I still feel that way. I never fail to experience their sense of joy.

Acting without state funds, Neff—a sort of Renaissance man who researches Colonial-era species, taught himself the Latin flower names, cooks harvest banquets from the produce grown in the garden, and serves it on dishes he throws and bakes in his home kiln—has turned what was once known as the Zambarano "Mud Hole" into the showplace of northern Rhode Island.

And he has given people who call an institution home a reason to live.

Zambarano, built in 1905 as a tuberculosis hospital and now a center for the elderly, disabled, and for people with spinal cord injuries or Alzheimer's disease, is of that old-fashioned dark-red brick school of institutional architecture. At its best it seems imposing; at its worst, dreary. But not anymore. Not since Peter Neff rolled up his sleeves and started digging. Finally persuading reluctant officials that the gardens wouldn't cost anything and that they'd be aesthetically beneficial, even to those who could only view them from the

**"IT IS NOTHING SHORT OF STUNNING
TO WALK ALONG THE PATHS. . ."**

window of a ward, Peter set about creating themed gardens.

He sculpted an English cottage garden, perennial borders, wildflower beds, water garden, and rose bowers, including flowers known to attract birds and butterflies and awaken memories in the hospital's patients. He planted the most aromatic plants to stir patients' senses but also made sure everything was nontoxic to accommodate the large number of Alzheimer's patients who might be inclined to taste.

The beds are bordered by huge rocks that Peter found in the surrounding woods and rolled out by hand; walkways are made of bricks salvaged from demolished buildings. The soil is enriched by compost made from the hospital's kitchen waste.

It is nothing short of stunning to walk along the paths designed for wheelchairs and drink in the palette of colors played out in poppies, sweet William, a half-dozen fragrant kinds of mint, bachelor's buttons, the exotic bee balm, pinks, meadow rue, Canterbury bells, irises, the fluffy-headed angelica and, beside a small pond Peter made, a Japanese water plant the size of Godzilla that was started six years earlier from a root bought at the Arnold Arboretum rare plant auction.

(The pond is its own challenge: It leaks. "Every year I have to drain it, find the leak and patch it, then fill it again," says Peter, with a faint sigh of self-reproach.)

All of the Zambarano gardeners are wheelchair-bound, some of them paralyzed in accidents, others handicapped by such illnesses as cerebral palsy and multiple sclerosis; some are stroke survivors. All of them are wildly enthusiastic about the gardens. They love to greet their visitors in the quiet beauty of the flower gardens or meet each other out there to share a snack or coffee.

But it's in the vegetable garden that they really excel, their imaginations knowing no bounds. They have complete responsibility for their individual plots, planted in raised beds for easy access; and those who have more difficulty controlling pair up to help each other. Working from their wheelchairs, they go about their tasks using special tools devised by the hospital's physical therapists.

The gardeners spend the winter months doing research to decide what to grow, meeting three times a week to view videos, hear guest lectures, and sketch plans. When spring comes, they rush outdoors to start their favorite cycle of activities: planting, weeding—Yes, they even love that!—and harvesting.

A large communal garden, tended by Neff, is the result of much group effort. The only fruit and vegetables ever considered for this space are the heirloom varieties, those whose beginnings can be traced to Colonial America. The most recent addition is a completely wheelchair-accesible garden containing heirloom apples, pears, plums, raspberries, blueberries, strawberries, and gooseberries.

The vegetable-growing efforts continue at such a high rate of production that the class can't consume all its crop. "We've been operating on a 'use it or lose it' basis," says Peter, who notes that, as a fundraising effort to subsidize further planting, the group has sold produce to the hospital staff since the first harvest. Now a small kitchen has been installed so the group can expand to canning and freezing fruit and vegetables for yummy meals during the long winter months.

During my most recent visit the beds were full of many types of squash including Boston marow, turks turban, and bush scallop, soldier beans, brandwine tomatoes, six varieties of peppers, eggplant, Swiss chard, broccoli, melons, red cabbage, potatoes (red and white), and Old Wethersfield red onions.

"We had broccoli calzones made from our own broccoli last week," says Frank Beazley, 67, who has lived at Zambarano for 29 years, since being paralyzed in a fall. "They were fabulous." A former baker, Frank is the hospital's unofficial goodwill ambassador, a constantly cheerful man who is a born diplomat.

The vegetable gardens are by no means a well-kept secret. Last year at the prestigious Olde Sturbridge Village Agricultural Fair in Massachusetts, members took three Best of Show ribbons competing against growers from as far away as California. "We had to grow varieties of vegetables from before 1830," explains Peter. This was the first horicultural therapy group ever to enter the competition.

Even though most of the members have been with the program from the beginning nobody seems to be getting bored. If anything, they're keener than ever to try new things and expand their potential. "It gives them a passion in life," says Peter. "They get fired up, feel they're really part of something."

Terry Medberry, a longtime resident and prize-winning poet, remembers that, before he became wheelchair-bound, he enjoyed helping his parents around the yard. When his mobility became so restricted that he was forced to move to the hospital, Terry really felt a void in his life. And then the horticultural therapy program came along and he's a changed man. Two years ago his winter squash took the blue ribbon at Sturbridge.

"I can't wait to get outside first thing in the morning," he says. "I just love it—the vegetables and flowers. It's tremendous. I work, watch what the others are doing. I listen to all the information Pete has to share with us. And I'm spending time with good friends."

Frank agrees with all that Terry said, and more. "It was fun right from the start. There's so much spirit, so much life. There's enjoyment for the patients, relatives, families. I go up and talk to the visitors and they never saw anything so spectacular. Peter deserves a lot of credit."

Rita Saltonstall, who took a Best of Show and a blue ribbon at Sturbridge—she jokes they were for "best entertainer"—adds, "This is one big happy family. We all root for each other." There's a lot to root for. Recently members of the group took seven blue ribbons at a huge Grange fair in rural Rhode Island, defeating professional farmers.

Meanwhile, the horticulture therapy program continues to grow and blossom. "It's just in its infancy" in terms of the possibilities, says Peter Neff. "We're looking into manufacturing our own glazes for our pots." So far he's thrown crocks, lidded casseroles, deep dish pie plates, and a tureen that group members have glazed. As a class project, they designed a teapot that resembles an 1800s hot chocolate pot. They've also been making little flower pots in which they plan to start seedlings from the garden for sale at their harvest fair.

So far their biggest fan is the one they need: A. Kathryn Power, director of Rhode Island's Department of Mental Health, Retardation and Hospitals, the agency that oversees Zambarano. She generally visits the hospital every two weeks, finding the work there incredible. The patients, she says, "go on and on about the intellectual stimulation of thinking about planning a garden. They are now the ones who are pushing us." Because so many younger patients—many victims of car accidents—are arriving at the hospital for what will be a lifelong stay, Power sees the gardening program as a real benefit. "It's a real value to have meaningful activities. They have not come to the hospital to die; they come here to live."

Recently a social worker named Myra Greene, employed at the main unit of the Eleanor Slater Hospital undertook to start a garden in the courtyard there in much the same spirit as Peter Neff's work at Zambarano. Last summer it was a profusion of blooms for the first garden party the hospital's ever had. Greene designed the garden herself—it is planted so that very tall flowers such as ruby canna lilies, feathery cleomes, and sunflowers—can be seen by patients even if they're being wheeled down the corridor on stretchers. As their Zambarano counterparts had done in following Neff's lead, a number of Slater staffers volunteered time and brought in gifts of plants to make the project a success.

The hospital soon will be getting another very special gift: The Zambarano horticultural therapy group is going to donate ten small trees from the collection on its lake-front grounds.

As usual Frank Beazley knows exactly what to say to express what the gardening program means at Zambarano, and what it is starting to mean at Eleanor Slater.

"It's the best thing in the world," he says. "The fresh air, the smell of the flowers. It's rewarding every day. It's

"I'LL TAKE YOU TO A PLACE WHERE
THERE IS NO ROOM FOR DESPAIR. . ."

a great, great group and we have our hearts and souls in it. We can go out there and have the fun we want. I'm very grateful for the opportunities we have here. It's such an open field now of handicapped people doing their thing."

So if you're ever having one of those "poor me" days when life has lost all meaning just give me a call. I'll take you to a place where there is no room for despair because everyone is too busy creating beauty.

It is the truest victory garden I know.